SELECTED POETRY OF AMIRI BARAKA/ LEROI JONES

SELECTED POETRY OF AMIRI BARAKA/ LEROI JONES

WILLIAM MORROW AND COMPANY, INC.
NEW YORK   1979

Copyright © 1979 by Amiri Baraka

Grateful acknowledgment is made for permission to use material as specified below:

From *Preface to a Twenty Volume Suicide Note,* Copyright © 1961 by LeRoi Jones, A Totem/Corinth Book, Corinth Books, Inc., 228 Everit Street, New Haven, Conn. 06511

From *The Dead Lecturer,* Copyright © 1963, 1964, 1965, 1967 by LeRoi Jones, Grove Press, Inc., New York, N.Y.

From *It's Nation Time,* Third World Press, 7524 South Cottage Grove, Chicago, Illinois 60619.

All rights reserved. No part of this book may be reproduced or utilized in any form or by any means, electronic or mechanical, including photocopying, recording or by any information storage and retrieval system, without permission in writing from the Publisher. Inquiries should be addressed to William Morrow and Company, Inc., 105 Madison Ave., New York, N. Y. 10016.

Library of Congress Cataloging in Publication Data

Baraka, Imamu Amiri, 1934-
  Selected poetry of Amiri Baraka/LeRoi Jones.

  I. Title.
PS3552.A583A17 1979   811'.5'4   79-9488
ISBN 0-688-03496-9
ISBN 0-688-08496-6 pbk.
Printed in the United States of America.

First Edition
1 2 3 4 5 6 7 8 9 10

For Amina Baraka, my wife
& Obalaji
   Ras Jua
   Shani
   Amiri
   Ahi, our children

CONTENTS

PREFACE TO A TWENTY VOLUME SUICIDE NOTE   *1*
Preface to a Twenty Volume Suicide Note   *2*
Hymn for Lanie Poo   *3*
In Memory of Radio   *9*
Look for You Yesterday, Here You Come Today   *10*
The Turncoat   *14*
The Insidious Dr. Fu Manchu   *15*
Notes for a Speech   *16*
THE DEAD LECTURER   *17*
For Edward Dorn   *18*
A contract. (for the destruction and rebuilding of Paterson   *19*
An Agony. As Now.   *20*
A Poem for Willie Best   *22*
The politics of rich painters   *28*
Rhythm & Blues (1   *30*
Crow Jane   *34*
For Crow Jane   *35*
Crow Jane's Manner.   *36*
Crow Jane in High Society.   *37*
Crow Jane the Crook.   *38*
The dead lady canonized   *39*
BLACK DADA NIHILISMUS   *40*
Political Poem   *43*
A Poem for Speculative Hipsters   *44*
The Liar   *45*
BLACK ART   *47*
Live Niggers—Stop Bullshitting   *48*
Salik   *49*

BLACK MAGIC *51*
Sabotage *53*
  Three Modes of History and Culture *53*
  A POEM SOME PEOPLE WILL HAVE TO UNDERSTAND *55*
  Houdini *56*
  Letter to E. Franklin Frazier *57*
  THE PEOPLE BURNING *58*
  Kenyatta Listening to Mozart *60*
  The New World *61*
  HEGEL *62*
  LEADBELLY GIVES AN AUTOGRAPH *64*
  Tone Poem *66*
  Loku *67*
  History As Process *68*
  DAVID COPPERHEAD *69*
  The Bronze Buckaroo *70*
Target Study *71*
  Numbers, Letters *71*
  Y O U N G S O U L *73*
  Confirmation *74*
  Friday *75*
  Here He Comes Again *76*
  I don't love you *77*
  Will They Cry When You're Gone, You Bet *78*
  What am I offered *79*
  Cold Term II *80*
  Sad Cowboy *81*
  Blue Whitie *82*
  Premises Not Quite Condemned *83*
  Red Eye *84*
  Lowdown *85*
  Western Front *86*
  20th-Century Fox *87*
  Poem *88*
  Reading and Weeping *89*
  Poem for Religious Fanatics *90*
  Precise Techniques *91*
  Cold Term *92*
  Jitterbugs *93*
  Word from the Right Wing *94*

NEWSHIT	95
Song	96
Lady Bug	97
THREE MOVEMENTS AND A CODA	98
T. T. Jackson sings	100
Return of the Native	101
Goodbye!	102
Black Bourgeoisie,	103
A Poem for Black Hearts	104
Black Art	105
SOS	105
Black Art	106
For a lady I know.	108
Poem for HalfWhite College Students	109
A School of Prayer	110
Biography	111
Red light	112
Little Brown Jug	113
W. W.	114
CIVIL RIGHTS POEM	115
the deadly eyes are stars!	116
Ka 'Ba	117
Beautiful Black Women...	118
Babylon Revisited	119
M a d n e s s	120
Bludoo Baby Want Money and Alligator Got It to Give	123
Stirling Street September	126
cops	127
The World Is Full of Remarkable Things	128
From the Egyptian	130
Election Day	132
leroy	134
Black People!	135
TENZI YA IMAMU	137
CENSUS	138
Wig Poem	139
Child Evolve	140
the boogaloo sonnet(s)	141
FUNKY BUTT, AN AMERICAN NEGRO MISSED-EQUAL PUET	142

Influence of	*144*
The Dance of the Toms	146
Time factor a perfect non-gap	*147*
No matter, No matter, the World Is the World	*148*
Prayer for Saving	150
Folks.	*153*
Who will survive America	155
Few Americans	
Very few Negroes	
No crackers at all.	
Reality is dealt with	*157*
"Dazed and out of their wool heads . . ."	*158*
Whas gon happen	*160*
In the Year	*162*
For Maulana Karenga & Pharoah Sanders	*163*
(Priest Poem)	*164*
NOTHING MORE TO SAY	*165*
OCTOBER 1969	*166*
Ask Me What I Am	*168*
NIXON	*169*
The Metropolis of Depraved Beings	*170*
Tanguhpay	*171*
We Are Here	*172*
Interest Circulating	*173*
Why didnt he tell me the whole truth	*174*
Africa Africa Africa	*175*
THE WORLD IS MY POEM	*177*
Bunnies	*178*
Profound is lost like everything else	*180*
CAREERS	*182*
The minute of consciousness	*183*
What are You waiting for?	*184*
THE STORY OF THE BLACK MAN IS A FUNNY STORY	*185*
Reality	*187*
IT'S NATION TIME	*189*
The Nation Is Like Ourselves	*190*
Sermon for Our Maturity	*193*
It's Nation Time	*198*
SPIRIT REACH	*201*
Deranged gutbucket pigtongue clapper heart.	*202*

STUDY PEACE	204
PEACE IN PLACE	205
COME SEE ABOUT ME	209
ALL IN THE STREET	211
JIM BROWN ON THE SCREEN	216
LOVE IS THE PRESENCE OF NO ENEMY	218
BAD NEWS FOR YOUR HIGHNESS (Song to Deposed Kings)	220
SOMEBODY'S SLOW IS ANOTHER BODY'S FAST (Preachment)	221
KUTOA UMOJA	224
THE SPIRIT OF CREATION IS BLACKNESS	225
SNAPSHOTS OF EVERYTHING	227
AFRIKAN REVOLUTION	229
AFRIKAN REVOLUTION	230
HARD FACTS	235
Introduction	236
Revolutionary Love	241
WATERGATE	242
When We'll Worship Jesus	243
Niggy the Ho	246
History on Wheels	248
CLAY	250
Rockefeller is yo vice president, & yo mamma dont wear no drawers	251
TODAY	252
Gibson	255
REAL LIFE	257
Red Autumn	258
AT THE NATIONAL BLACK ASSEMBLY	259
3RD WORLD BLUES	261
A New Reality Is Better Than a New Movie!	262
The Dictatorship of the Proletariat	263
Das Kapital	266
A POEM FOR DEEP THINKERS	267
Class Struggle	269
For the Revolutionary Outburst by Black People	271
POETRY FOR THE ADVANCED	275
Introduction	276
A POEM FOR ANNA RUSS AND FANNY JONES	277
Sayonara, Tokyo	278

Reprise of One of A.G.'s Best Poems!	*280*
MALCOLM REMEMBERED (FEB. '77)	*287*
AN AMERICAN OPPRESS STORY!	*293*
LIKE, THIS IS WHAT I MEANT!	*294*
The "Race Line" Is a Product of Capitalism	*298*
ALL REACTION IS DOOMED!!!	*307*
Chinatown	*317*
On the Money	*319*
Pres Spoke in a Language	*320*
Inside Out	*321*
Afro-American Lyric	*322*
Spring Song	*328*
Dope	*329*
Am/Trak	*332*
Child of the Thirties	*338*

PREFACE TO A TWENTY VOLUME SUICIDE NOTE

PREFACE TO A TWENTY VOLUME SUICIDE NOTE

(For Kellie Jones, born 16 May 1959)

Lately, I've become accustomed to the way
The ground opens up and envelops me
Each time I go out to walk the dog.
Or the broad edged silly music the wind
Makes when I run for a bus...

Things have come to that.

And now, each night I count the stars,
And each night I get the same number.
And when they will not come to be counted,
I count the holes they leave.

Nobody sings anymore.

And then last night, I tiptoed up
To my daughter's room and heard her
Talking to someone, and when I opened
The door, there was no one there...
Only she on her knees, peeking into

Her own clasped hands.

March 1957

HYMN FOR LANIE POO

Vous êtes de faux Nègres
    —Rimbaud

O,
these wild trees
will make charming wicker baskets,
the young woman
the young black woman
the young black beautiful woman
said.
  These wild-assed trees
  will make charming
  wicker baskets.

(now, I'm putting words in her mouth . . . tch)

1

All afternoon
we watched the cranes
humping each other
     dropped
     our shadows
     onto the beach
and covered them over with sand.

Beware the evil sun . . .
turn you black

turn your hair

crawl your eyeballs

rot your teeth.

All afternoon
we sit around
near the edge of the city
     hacking open
     crocodile skulls
     sharpening our teeth.

The god I pray to
got black boobies
got steatopygia

make faces in the moon
make me a greenpurple &
maroon winding sheet.
                    I wobble out to
                    the edge of the water

give my horny yell
& 24 elephants
stomp out of the subway
with consecrated hardons.

(watch out for that evil sun
turn you black)
            My fireface

my orange
and fireface
squat by the flames.
She had her coming out party
with 3000 guests
from all parts of the country.
Queens, Richmond, Togoland, The Cameroons;
A white hunter, very unkempt,
with long hair,
whizzed in on the end of a vine.
(spoke perfect english too.)

"Throw on another goddamned Phoenician,"
I yelled, really getting with it.

John Coltrane arrived with an Egyptian lady.
he played very well.

"Throw on another goddamned Phoenician."

We got so drunk (Hulan Jack
brought his bottle of Thunderbird),
nobody went hunting
the next morning.

4 /

2

o,
don't be shy honey.
we all know
these wicker baskets
would make wild-assed trees.

Monday, I spent most of the day hunting.
Knocked off about six, gulped down a couple of monkey foreskins, then took in a
flick. Got to bed early.

Tuesday, same thing all day. (Caught a
mangy lioness with one tit.) Ate.
Watched television for awhile. Read the
paper, then hit the sack.

Wednesday, took the day off.
Took the wife and kids to the games.
Read Garmanda's book, "14 Tribes of
Ambiguity," didn't like it.

Thursday, we caught a goddamn ape.
Must've weighed about 600 pounds.
We'll probably eat ape meat for the
rest of the month. Christ, I hate
ape meat.

Friday, I stayed home with a supposed
cold. Goofed the whole day trying to
rethatch the roof. Had run in with
the landlord.

We spent the weekend at home.
I tried to get some sculpting done,
but nothing came of it. It's impossible to be an artist and a bread
winner at the same time.
Sometimes I think I oughta chuck
the whole business.

3

The firemasons parade.

(The sun is using this country
as a commode.

Beware the sun, my love.)

The firemasons are very square.
They are supposed to be a civic
and fraternal organization, but
all they do is have parades and
stay high. They also wear funny
looking black hats, which are
round and have brims. The fire-
masons are cornballs.

4

Each morning
I go down
to Gansevoort St.
and stand on the docks.
I stare out
at the horizon
until it gets up
and comes to embrace
me. I
make believe
it is my father.
This is known
as genealogy.

5

We came into the
silly little church
shaking our wet raincoats
on the floor.
It wasn't water,
that made the raincoats
wet.

The preacher's
conning eyes
fired when he saw
the way I walked to-
wards him; almost
throwing my hips out
of whack.
He screamed,

He's wet with the blood of the lamb!!

And everybody
got real happy.

       6 (die schwartze Bohemein)

They laught,

and religion was something

he fount in coffee shops, by God.

It's not that I got enything

against cotton, nosiree, by God

It's just that . . .
    Man lookatthatblonde
         , whewee!

I think they are not treating us like

Mr. Lincun said they should
      or Mr. Gandhi

For that matter. By God.

     ZEN

is a bitch! Like "Bird" was,
     Cafe Olay

for me, Miss.

>   But white cats can't swing ...

Or the way this guy kept patronizing me—

like he was Bach or somebody

>   Oh, I knew

John Kasper when he hung around with shades ...

>   She's a painter, Man.

It's just that it's such a drag to go

Way uptown for Bar B Cue,
>   By God ...

How much?

7

About my sister.
>   (O, generation revered
>   above all others.
>   O, generation of fictitious
>   Ofays
>   I revere you ...
>   You are all so beautiful)

my sister drives a green jaguar
my sister has her hair done twice a month
my sister is a school teacher
my sister took ballet lessons
my sister has a fine figure: never diets
my sister doesn't like to teach in Newark
   because there are too many colored
   in her classes
my sister hates loud shades
my sister's boy friend is a faggot music teacher
   who digs Tschaikovsky
my sister digs Tschaikovsky also

IN MEMORY OF RADIO

Who has ever stopped to think of the divinity of Lamont Cranston?
(Only Jack Kerouac, that I know of: & me.
The rest of you probably had on WCBS and Kate Smith,
Or something equally unattractive.)

What can I say?
It is better to have loved and lost
Than to put linoleum in your living rooms?

Am I a sage or something?
Mandrake's hypnotic gesture of the week?
(Remember, I do not have the healing powers of Oral Roberts . . .
I cannot, like F. J. Sheen, tell you how to get saved & *rich!*
I cannot even order you to gaschamber satori like Hitler or
    Goody Knight

& Love is an evil word.
Turn it backwards/see, see what I mean?
An evol word. & besides
who understands it?
I certainly wouldn't like to go out on that kind of limb.

Saturday mornings we listened to *Red Lantern* & his undersea folk.
At 11, *Let's Pretend*/& we did/&I, the poet, still do, Thank God!

What was it he used to say (after the transformation, when he was safe
& invisible & the unbelievers couldn't throw stones?) "Heh, heh, heh,
Who knows what evil lurks in the hearts of men? The Shadow knows."

O, yes he does
O, yes he does.
An evil word it is,
This Love.

LOOK FOR YOU YESTERDAY, HERE YOU COME TODAY

Part of my charm:
        envious blues feeling
        separation of church & state
        grim calls from drunk debutantes

Morning never aids me in my quest.
I have to trim my beard in solitude.
I try to hum lines from "The Poet In New York."

People saw metal all around the house on Saturdays. The Phone
                                                                            rings.

terrible poems come in the mail. Descriptions of celibate parties
        torn trousers: Great Poets dying
        with their strophes on. & me
        incapable of a simple straightforward
        anger.

It's so diffuse
being alive. Suddenly one is aware
        that nobody really gives a damn.
        My wife is pregnant with *her* child.
        "It means nothing to me," sez Strindberg.

An avalanche of words
could cheer me up. Words from Great Sages.
        Was James Karolis a great sage??
        Why did I let Ora Matthews beat him up
        in the bathroom? Haven't I learned my lesson.

I would take up painting
if I cd think of a way to do it
better than Leonardo. Than Bosch.
Than Hogarth. Than Kline.

Frank walked off the stage, singing
"My silence is as important as Jack's incessant yatter."

I am a mean hungry sorehead
Do I have the capacity for grace??

To arise one smoking spring
& find one's youth has taken off
for greener parts.

A sudden blankness in the day
as if there were no afternoon.
& all my piddling joys retreated
to their own dopey mythic worlds.

The hours of the atmosphere
grind their teeth like hags.

    (When will world war two be over?)

I stood up on a mailbox
waving my yellow tee-shirt
watching the gray tanks
stream up Central Ave.

    All these thots
    are Flowers Of Evil
    cold & lifeless
    as subway rails

the sun like a huge cobblestone
flaking its brown slow rays
primititi
   once, twice. My life
   seems over & done with.
   Each morning I rise
   like a sleep walker
   & rot a little more.

All the lovely things I've known have disappeared.
I have all my pubic hair & am lonely.
There is probably no such place as BattleCreek, Michigan!

Tom Mix dead in a Boston Nightclub
before I realized what happened.

People laugh when I tell them about Dickie Dare!

What is one to do in an alien planet
where the people breathe New Ports?
Where is my space helmet, I sent for it
3 lives ago . . . when there were box tops.

What has happened to box tops??

O, God . . . I must have a belt that glows green
in the dark. Where is my Captain Midnight decoder??
I can't understand what Superman is saying!

   THERE *MUST* BE A LONE RANGER!!!

           *   *   *   *

but this also
is part of my charm.
A maudlin nostalgia
that comes on
like terrible thoughts about death.

How dumb to be sentimental about anything
To call it love
& cry pathetically
into the long black handkerchief
of the years.

        "Look for you yesterday
        Here you come today
        Your mouth wide open
        But what you got to say?"

            —part of my charm

                old envious   blues feeling
                ticking like   a big cobblestone clock.

I hear the reel running out . . .
the spectators are impatient for popcorn:
It was only a selected short subject

F. Scott Charon
will soon be glad-handing me
like a legionnaire

My silver bullets all gone
My black mask trampled in the dust

& Tonto way off in the hills
moaning like Bessie Smith.

THE TURNCOAT

The steel fibrous slant & ribboned glint
of water. The Sea. Even my secret speech is moist
with it. When I am alone & brooding, locked in
with dull memories & self hate, & the terrible disorder
of a young man.

I move slowly. My cape spread stiff & pressing cautiously
in the first night wind off the Hudson. I glide down
onto my own roof, peering in at the pitiful shadow of myself.

How can it mean anything? The stop & spout, the
wind's dumb shift. Creak of the house & wet smells
coming in. Night forms on my left. The blind still
up to admit a sun that no longer exists. Sea move.

I dream long bays & towers . . . & soft steps on moist sand.
I become them, sometimes. Pure fight. Pure fantasy. Lean.

THE INSIDIOUS DR. FU MANCHU

If I think myself
strong, then I am
not true to the misery
in my life. The uncertainty.
(of what I am saying, who
I have chose to become, the
very air pressing my skin
held gently away, this woman
and the one I taste continually
in my nebular pallet tongue face
mouth feet, standing in piles
of numbers, hills, lovers.
                              If

I think myself ugly
& go to the mirror, smiling,
at the inaccuracy, or Now
the rain pounds dead grass
in the stone yard, I think
how very wise I am. How very
very wise.

NOTES FOR A SPEECH

African blues
does not know me. Their steps, in sands
of their own
land. A country
in black & white, newspapers
blown down pavements
of the world. Does
not feel
what I am.
        Strength
in the dream, an oblique
suckling of nerve, the wind
throws up sand, eyes
are something locked in
hate, of hate, of hate, to
walk abroad, they conduct
their deaths apart
from my own. Those
heads, I call
my "people."
        (And who are they. People. To concern
myself, ugly man. Who
you, to concern
the white flat stomachs
of maidens, inside houses
dying. Black. Peeled moon
light on my fingers
move under
her clothes. Where
is her husband. Black
words throw up sand
to eyes, fingers of
their private dead. Whose
soul, eyes, in sand. My color
is not theirs. Lighter, white man
talk. They shy away. My own
dead souls, my, so called
people. Africa
is a foreign place. You are
as any other sad man here
american.

THE
DEAD
LECTURER

FOR EDWARD DORN

"In blackest day, In blackest night
No evil shall escape my sight!
Let those who worship evil's might
Beware my power...
Green Lantern's Light."

A CONTRACT. (FOR THE DESTRUCTION AND REBUILDING OF PATERSON

Flesh, and cars, tar, dug holes beneath stone
a rude hierarchy of money, band saws cross out
music, feeling. Even speech, corrodes.
                                            I came here
from where I sat boiling in my veins, cold fear
at the death of men, the death of learning, in
cold fear, at my own. Romantic vests of same death
blank at the corner, blank when they raise their fingers

Criss the hearts, in dark flesh staggered so marvelous
are their lies. So complete, their mastery, of these
stupid niggers. Loud spics kill each other, and will not

make the simple trip to Tiffany's. Will not smash their stainless
heads, against the simpler effrontery of so callous a code as gain.

You are no brothers, dirty woogies, dying under dried rinds, in
    massa's
droopy tuxedos. Cab Calloways of the soul, at the soul's juncture,
    a
music, they think will save them from our eyes. (In back of the
    terminal

where the circus will not go. At the backs of crowds, stooped
    and vulgar
breathing hate syllables, unintelligible rapes of all that linger in
our new world. Killed in white fedora hats, they stand so mute
    at what

whiter slaves did to my fathers. They muster silence. They pray
    at the
steps of abstract prisons, to be kings, when all is silence, when all
is stone. When even the stupid fruit of their loins is gold, or
    something
else they cannot eat.

AN AGONY. AS NOW.

I am inside someone
who hates me. I look
out from his eyes. Smell
what fouled tunes come in
to his breath. Love his
wretched women.

Slits in the metal, for sun. Where
my eyes sit turning, at the cool air
the glance of light, or hard flesh
rubbed against me, a woman, a man,
without shadow, or voice, or meaning.

This is the enclosure (flesh,
where innocence is a weapon. An
abstraction. Touch. (Not mine,
Or yours, if you are the soul I had
and abandoned when I was blind and had
my enemies carry me as a dead man
(if he is beautiful, or pitied.

It can be pain. (As now, as all his
flesh hurts me.) It can be that. Or
pain. As when she ran from me into
·that forest.
        Or pain, the mind
silver spiraled whirled against the
sun, higher than even old men thought
God would be. Or pain. And the other. The
yes. (Inside his books, his fingers. They
are withered yellow flowers and were never
beautiful.) The yes. You will, lost soul, say
'beauty.' Beauty, practiced, as the tree. The
slow river. A white sun in its wet sentences.

Or, the cold men in their gale. Ecstasy. Flesh
or soul. The yes. (Their robes blown. Their bowls
empty. They chant at my heels, not at yours.) Flesh
or soul, as corrupt. Where the answer moves too quickly.
Where the God is a self, after all.)

Cold air blown through narrow blind eyes. Flesh,
white hot metal. Glows as the day with its sun.
It is a human love, I live inside. A bony skeleton
you recognize as words or simple feeling.

But it has no feeling. As the metal, is hot, it is not,
given to love.

It burns the thing
inside it. And that thing
screams.

A POEM FOR WILLIE BEST *

I

The face sings, alone
at the top
          of the body. All
flesh, all song, aligned. For hell
is silent, at those cracked lips
flakes of skin and mind
twist and whistle softly
as they fall.
          It was your own death
you saw. Your own face, stiff
and raw. This
without sound, or
movement. Sweet afton, the
dead beggar bleeds
yet. His blood, for a time
alive, and huddled in a door
way, struggling to sing. Rain
washes it into cracks. Pits
whose bottoms are famous. Whose sides
are innocent broadcasts
of another life.

II

At this point, neither
front nor back. A point, the
dimensionless line. The top
of a head, seen from Christ's
heaven, stripped of history
or desire.
          Fixed, perpendicular
to shadow. (even speech, vertical,
leaves no trace. Born in to death
held fast to it, where
the lover spreads his arms, the line
he makes to threaten Gods with history.

* Willie Best was a negro character actor whose Hollywood name was Sleep'n'eat.

The fingers stretch to emptiness. At
each point, after flesh, even light
is speculation. But an end, his end,
failing a beginning.

2

A cross. The gesture, symbol, line
arms held stiff, nailed stiff, with
no sign, of what gave them strength.
The point, become a line, a cross, or
the man, and his material, driven in
the ground. If the head rolls back
and the mouth opens, screamed into
existence, there will be perhaps
only the slightest hint of movement—
a smear; no help will come. No one
will turn to that station again.

III

At a cross roads, sits the
player. No drum, no umbrella, even
though it's raining. Again, and we
are somehow less miserable because
here is a hero, used to being wet.
One road is where you are standing now
(reading this, the other, crosses then
rushes into a wood.
         5 lbs neckbones.
         5 lbs hog innards.
        10 bottles cheap wine.
                (the contents
of a paper bag, also shoes, with holes
for the big toe, and several rusted
knives. This is a literature, of
symbols. And it is his gift, as the
bag is.
    (The contents
again, holy saviours,

/ 23

                        300 men on horseback
                        75 bibles
                        the quietness
of a field. A rich
man, though wet through
by the rain.
            I said,
                        47 howitzers
                        7 polished horse jaws
                        a few trees being waved
softly back under
the black night
                        All This sould be
invested.

IV

Where
ever,
        he has gone. Who ever
mourns
or sits silent
to remember

There is nothing of pity
here. Nothing
of sympathy.

V

This is the dance of the raised
leg. Of the hand on the knee
quickly.
            As a dance it punishes
speech. 'The house burned. The
old man killed.'
                    As a dance it
is obscure.

VI

This is the song
of the highest C.
                    The falsetto. An elegance

that punishes silence. This is the song
of the toes pointed inward, the arms swung, the
hips, moved, for fucking, slow, from side
to side. He is quote
saying, "My father was
never a jockey,
        but
                he did teach me
                how to ride."

VII

The balance.
            (Rushed in, swarmed of dark, cloaks,
and only red lights pushed a message
to the street. Rub.
                This is the lady,
I saw you with.
This is your mother.
This is the lady I wanted
some how to sleep with.
                    As a dance, or
our elegant song. Sun red and grown
from trees, fences, mud roads in dried out
river beds. This is for me, with no God
but what is given. Give me
                    Something more
than what is here. I must tell you
my body hurts.

The balance.
              Can you hear? Here
I am again. Your boy, dynamite. Can
you hear? My soul is moved. The soul
you gave me. I say, my soul, and it
is moved. That soul
you gave me.
              Yes, I'm sure
this is the lady. You
slept with her. Witness, your boy,
here, dynamite. Hear?
                I mean
can you?

The balance.
           He was tired of losing. (And
his walking buddies tired
of walking.
          Bent slightly,
at the waist. Left hand low, to flick
quick showy jabs ala Sugar. The right
cocked, to complete,
                  any combination.
                          He was
tired of losing, but he was fighting
a big dumb "farmer."
                Such a blue bright
afternoon, and only a few hundred yards
from the beach. He said, I'm tired
of losing.
        "I *got* ta cut'cha."

VIII

A renegade
behind the mask. And even
the mask, a renegade
disguise. Black skin
and hanging lip.
          Lazy
          Frightened
          Thieving
          Very potent sexually
          Scars
          Generally inferior
                    (but natural

rhythms.

His head is
at the window. The only
part
    that sings.

(The word he used
                (we are passing St. Mark's place
                and those crazy jews who fuck)
                                  to provoke

in neon, still useful
in the rain,
            to provoke
some meaning, where before
there was only hell. I said
silence, at his huddled blood.
                    It is an obscene invention.
                    A white sticky discharge.
                    "Jism," in white chalk
                    on the back of Angel's garage.
                    Red jackets with the head of
                    Hobbes staring into space. "Jasm"
                    the name the leader took, had it
                    stenciled on his chest.
                              And he sits
wet at the crossroads, remembering distinctly
each weightless face that eases by. (Sun at
the back door, and that hideous mindless grin.
                              (Hear?

THE POLITICS OF RICH PAINTERS

is something like the rest
of our doubt, whatever slow thought
comes to rest, beneath the silence
of starving talk.
                Just their fingers' prints
staining the cold glass, is sufficient
for commerce, and a proper ruling on
humanity. You know the pity
of democracy, that we must sit here
and listen to how he made his money.
Tho the catalogue of his possible ignorance
roars and extends through the room
like fire. "Love," becomes the pass,
the word taken intimately to combat
all the uses of language. So that learning
itself falls into disrepute.

2.

What they have gathered into themselves
in that short mean trip from mother's iron tit
to those faggot handmaidens of the french whore
who wades slowly in the narrows, waving her burnt out
torch. There are movies, and we have opinions. There are
regions of compromise so attractive, we daily long
to filthy our minds with their fame. And all the songs
of our handsome generation fall clanging like stones
in the empty darkness of their heads.
                                  Couples, so beautiful
in the newspapers, marauders of cheap sentiment. So much *taste*
so little understanding, except some up and coming queer explain
cinema and politics while drowning a cigarette.

3.

They are more ignorant than the poor
tho they pride themselves with that accent. And
move easily in fake robes of egalitarianism. Meaning,
I will fuck you even if you don't like art. And are wounded
that you call their italian memories petit bourgeois.

           Whose death
will be Malraux's? Or the names Senghor, Price, Baldwin
whispered across the same dramatic pancakes, to let each eyelash
  flutter
at the news of their horrible deaths. It is a cheap game
to patronize the dead, unless their deaths be accountable
to your own understanding. Which be nothing nothing
if not bank statements and serene trips to our ominous country-
  side.
Nothing, if not whining talk about handsome white men. Nothing
if not false glamorous and static. Except, I admit, your lives
are hideously real.

4.

The source of their art crumbles into legitimate history.
The whimpering pigment of a decadent economy, slashed into
  life
as Yeats' mad girl plummeting over the nut house wall, her broken
knee caps rattling in the weather, reminding us of lands
our antennae do not reach.

And there are people in these savage geographies
use your name in other contexts
think, perhaps, the title of your latest painting
another name for liar.

RHYTHM & BLUES (1
(for Robert Williams, in exile)

The symbols hang limply
in the street. A forest of objects,
motives,
       black steaming christ
       meat wood and cars
       flesh light and stars
       scream each new dawn for

whatever leaves pushed from gentle lips
fire shouted from the loins of history
immense dream of each silence grown to punctuation
against the gray flowers of the world.

    I live against them, and hear them, and move
the way they move. Hanged against the night, so many
leaves, not even moving. The women scream tombs
and give the nights a dignity. For his heels
dragged in the brush. For his lips dry as brown wood. As
the simple motion of flesh whipping the air.

An incorrigible motive.
An action so secret it creates.
Men dancing on a beach.
Disappeared laughter erupting as the sea
erupts.
Controlled eyes seeing now all
there is
Ears that have grown
to hold their new maps
Enemies that grow
in silence
Empty white fingers
against the keys (a drunken foolish stupor
to kill these men
and scream "Economics," my God, "Economics"
for all the screaming women drunker still, laid out to rest
under the tables of nightclubs
under the thin trees of expensive forests
informed of nothing save the stink of their failure

the peacock insolence of zombie regimes
the diaphanous silence of empty churches
the mock solitude of a spastic's art.
                               "Love." My God, (after they
scream "Economics," these shabby personalities
the pederast anarchist chants against millions of
Elk-sundays in towns quieter than his. Lunches. Smells
the sidewalk invents, and the crystal music even dumb niggers
hate. They scream it down. They will not hear your jazz. Or
let me tell of the delicate colors of the flag, the graphic blouse
of the beautiful italian maiden. Afternoon spas
with telephone booths, Butterfingers, grayhaired anonymous
      trustees
dying with the afternoon. The people of my life
caressed with a silence that only they understand. Let their sons
make wild sounds of their mothers for your pleasure. Or
drive deep wedges in flesh / screaming birds of morning, at
their own. The invisible mountains of New Jersey, linger
where I was born. And the wind on that stone

2)

Street of tinsel, and the jeweled dancers
of Belmont. Stone royalty they tear down
for new buildings where fags invent jellies.

A tub, a slick head, and the pink houses waving
at the night as it approaches. A dead fish truck
full of porters I ran track with, effeminate blues singers, the
      wealth
of the nation transposed into the ring of my flesh's image. Grand
      dancers
spray noise and disorder in these old tombs. Liverwurst sand-
      wiches dry
on brown fenced-in lawns, unfinished cathedrals tremble with our
      screams.
Of the dozens, the razor, the cloth, the sheen, all speed adventure
      locked

/ 31

in my eyes. I give you now, to love me, if I spare what flesh of
   yours
is left. If I see past what I feel, and call music simply "Art" and
   will
not take it to its logical end. For the death by hanging, for
the death by the hooded political murderer, for the old man dead
   in his
tired factory; election machines chime quietly his fraudulent faith.

For the well that marks the burned stores. For the deadly idiot
   of compromise
who shrieks compassion, and bids me love my neighbor. Even
   beyond the meaning
of such act as would give all my father's dead ash to fertilize
   their bilious
land. Such act as would give me legend, "This is the man who
   saved us
Spared us from the disappearance of the sixteenth note, the
   destruction
of the scale. This is the man who against the black pits of despair-
   ing genius
cried, "Save the Popular Song." For them who pat me in the
   huddle and do not
argue at the plays. For them who finish second and are happy
   they are Chinese,
and need not run those 13 blocks.

I am not moved. I will not move to save them. There is no
"melody." Only the foot stomped, the roaring harmonies of need.
   The
hand banged on the table, waved in the air. The teeth pushed
   against
the lip. The face and fingers sweating. "Let me alone," is praise
   enough
for these musicians.

3)

My own mode of conscience. And guilt, always the obvious
   connection.
They spread you in the sun, and leave you there, one of a kind,
   who

has no sons to tell this to. The mind so bloated at its own judg-
    ment. The
railing consequence of energy given in silence. Ideas whose sole
    place
is where they form. The language less than the act. The act so
    far beyond
itself, meaning all forms, all modes, all voices, chanting for safety.

I am deaf and blind and lost and will not again sing your quiet
    verse. I have lost
even the act of poetry, and writhe now for cool horizonless dawn.
    The
shake and chant, bulled electric motion, figure of what there will
    be
as it sits beside me waiting to live past my own meekness. My
    own
light skin. Bull of yellow perfection, imperfectly made, im-
    perfectly
understood, except as it rises against the mountains, like sun
but brighter, like flame but hotter. There will be those
who will tell you it will be beautiful.

CROW JANE

"Crow Jane, Crow Jane, don't hold your head so high,
You realize, baby, you got to lay down and die."
                              —Mississippi Joe Williams

FOR CROW JANE
        (Mama Death.

For dawn, wind
off the river. Wind
and light, from
the lady's hand. Cold
stuff, placed against
strong man's lips. Young gigolo's
of the 3rd estate. Young ruffians
without no homes. The wealth
is translated, corrected, a
dark process, like thought, tho
it provide a landscape
with golden domes.
                'Your people
without love.' And life
rots them. Makes a silence
blankness in every space
flesh thought to be. (First light,
is dawn. Cold stuff
to tempt a lover. Old lady
of flaking eyes. Moon lady
of useless thighs.

CROW JANE'S MANNER.
                    Is some pilgrimage

to thought. Where she goes, in fairness,
"nobody knows." And then, without love,
returns to those wrinkled stomachs
ragged bellies / of young ladies
gone with seed. Crow
will not have. Dead virgin
of the mind's echo. Dead lady
of thinking, back now, without
the creak of memory.
                    Field is yellow. Fils dead
(Me, the last . . . black lip hung
in dawn's gray wind. The last,
for love, a taker, took my kin.

Crow. Crow. Where
you leave my
other boys?

CROW JANE IN HIGH SOCIETY.
                    (Wipes

her nose
on the draperies. Spills drinks
fondles another man's
life. She is looking
for alternatives. Openings
where she can lay all
this greasy talk
on somebody. Me, once. Now
I am her teller.
            (And I tell
her symbols, as the gray movement
of clouds. Leave
gray movements
of clouds. Leave, always,
more.

Where is she? That she
moves without light. Even
in our halls. Even with
our laughter, lies, dead drunk
in a slouch hat famous king.
                    Where?

To come on so.

CROW JANE THE CROOK.

Of the night
of the rain, she
reigned, reined, her
fat whores and horse.

(A cloud burst,
and wet us. The mountain
split, and burned us. We thought
we were done.

               Jane.
Wet lady of no image. We
thought, you had left us. Dark
lady, of constant promise. We thought
you had gone.

2.

My heart is cast in bitter
metal. Condiments, spices
all the frustration of earth,
that has so much more desire

than resolution. Want than pleasure.
Oh, Jane. (Her boat bumps at the ragged
shore. Soul of the ocean, go out, return.
Oh, Jane, we thought you had gone.

THE DEAD LADY CANONIZED

                        (A thread
of meaning. Meaning light. The quick
response. To breath, or the virgins
sick odor against the night.

                        (A trail
of objects. Dead nouns, rotted faces
propose the night's image. Erect
for that lady, a grave of her own.

                        (The stem
of the morning, sets itself, on
each window (of thought, where it
goes. The lady is dead, may the Gods,

                        (those others
beg our forgiveness. And Damballah, kind father,
sew up
her bleeding hole.

BLACK DADA NIHILISMUS

. Against what light

is false what breath
sucked, for deadness.
                    Murder, the cleansed

purpose, frail, against
God, if they bring him
                    bleeding, I would not

forgive, or even call him
black dada nihilismus.

The protestant love, wide windows,
color blocked to Mondrian, and the
ugly silent deaths of jews under
the surgeon's knife. (To awake on
69th street with money and a hip
nose. Black dada nihilismus, for

the umbrella'd jesus. Trilby intrigue
movie house presidents sticky the floor.
B.D.N., for the secret men, Hermes, the

blacker art. Thievery (ahh, they return
those secret gold killers. Inquisitors
of the cocktail hour. Trismegistus, have

them, in their transmutation, from stone
to bleeding pearl, from lead to burning
looting, dead Moctezuma, find the West

a gray hideous space.

2.

From Sartre, a white man, it gave
the last breath. And we beg him die,
before he is killed. Plastique, we

do not have, only thin heroic blades.
The razor. Our flail against them, why
you carry knives? Or brutaled lumps of

heart? Why you stay, where they can
reach? Why you sit, or stand, or walk
in this place, a window on a dark

warehouse. Where the minds packed in
straw. New homes, these towers, for those
lacking money or art. A cult of death,

need of the simple striking arm under
the streetlamp. The cutters, from under
their rented earth. Come up, black dada

nihilismus. Rape the white girls. Rape
their fathers. Cut the mothers' throats.
Black dada nihilismus, choke my friends

in their bedrooms with their drinks spilling
and restless for tilting hips or dark liver
lips sucking splinters from the master's thigh.

Black scream
and chant, scream,
and dull, un
earthly

hollering. Dada, bilious
what ugliness, learned
in the dome, colored holy
shit (i call them sinned

or lost
       burned masters
              of the lost
                      nihil German killers
                                all our learned

art, 'member
what you said
money, God, power,
a moral code, so cruel
it destroyed Byzantium, Tenochtitlan, Commanch
                              (got it, *Baby!*

For tambo, willie best, dubois, patrice, mantan, the
bronze buckaroos.

                for Jack Johnson, asbestos, tonto, buckwheat,
                billie holiday.

                For tom russ, l'ouverture, vesey, beau jack,

(may a lost god damballah, rest or save us
against the murders we intend
against his lost white children
black dada nihilismus

POLITICAL POEM

(for Basil)

Luxury, then, is a way of
being ignorant, comfortably
An approach to the open market
of least information. Where theories
can thrive, under heavy tarpaulins
without being cracked by ideas.

(I have not seen the earth for years
and think now possibly "dirt" is
negative, positive, but clearly
social. I cannot plant a seed, cannot
recognize the root with clearer dent
than indifference. Though I eat
and shit as a natural man. (Getting up
from the desk to secure a turkey sandwich
and answer the phone: the poem undone
undone by my station, by my station,
and the bad words of Newark.) Raised up
to the breech, we seek to fill for this
crumbling century. The darkness of love,
in whose sweating memory all error is forced.

Undone by the logic of any specific death. (Old gentlemen
who still follow fires, tho are quieter
and less punctual. It is a polite truth
we are left with. Who are you? What are you
saying? Something to be dealt with, as easily.
The noxious game of reason, saying, "No, No,
you cannot feel," like my dead lecturer
lamenting thru gipsies his fast suicide.

A POEM FOR SPECULATIVE HIPSTERS

He had got, finally,
to the forest
of motives. There were no
owls, or hunters. No Connie Chatterleys
resting beautifully
on their backs, having casually
brought socialism
to England.
        Only ideas,
and their opposites.
                Like,
        he was *really*
        nowhere.

THE LIAR

What I thought was love
in me, I find a thousand instances
as fear. (Of the tree's shadow
winding around the chair, a distant music
of frozen birds rattling
in the cold.
        Where ever I go to claim
my flesh, there are entrances
of spirit. And even its comforts
are hideous uses I strain
to understand.
          Though I am a man
who is loud
on the birth
of his ways. Publicly redefining
each change in my soul, as if I had predicted
them,
    and profited, biblically, even tho
    their chanting weight,
            erased familiarity
            from my face.
                A question I think,
an answer; whatever sits
counting the minutes
till you die.

        When they say, "It is Roi
        who is dead?" I wonder
        who will they mean?

BLACK
ART

LIVE NIGGERS—STOP BULLSHITTING *

Disturb as dust falls happy young blood
walking in the owl club Ed Brooke style
a yankee No How, a kowtow to double
dutch anteaters, crotch charlie the freak
captain. disturb is change, over an',
out Blown Free, sweet blackness
took us back. Sweet black, & flying
high over devil land I know who
talks with God. A black man in
black inside skin. Say-Pop. Say Yeh
Pop pop. Say. Hey. Pop & Pop Pop
you got a terrible thing going brother
You got a really terrible thing going
(devil dropped a book on my head)
dont stand up please & sit back
down, keep on standin
& standin
& keep a really Black Thing
gogrroov beebeep
    Ah bee-bee
    Ah bee-bee
    Ah bee-bee
keep a real good strong healthy
fast intelligent groo-groovy black
thing goin

* First appeared in *Black Art* (Jihad, 1967)

SALIK *

The word is edged with fire. The word is
mine, and the lord that it is, is mine,
and the energy straight from god, this constant prayer
i give, is mine, and the eye thought you would see

the many levels of being
life itself is split into atoms
and each particle is a magnificent universe
full of good
and evil

i awake in the mad foolishness of crazy fucking a
                                          merica
white people are loose in the streets
we think about the ways to restore our gesture
and understanding, keeping the world natural
changing the nature of
moving in the actual spirit, its the time
ing
the
ri-
thum

in the constant gorgeous
reenactment of God re-
creating
himself

* First appeared in *Black Art* (Jihad, 1967)

BLACK
MAGIC

SABOTAGE

THREE MODES OF HISTORY AND CULTURE

Chalk mark sex of the nation, on walls we drummers
know
as cathedrals. Cathedra, in a churning meat milk.

Women glide through looking for telephones. Maps
weep
and are mothers and their daughters listening to

music teachers. From heavy beginnings. Plantations,
learning
America, as speech, and a common emptiness. Songs knocking

inside old women's faces. Knocking through cardboard trunks.
Trains
leaning north, catching hellfire in windows, passing through

the first ignoble cities of missouri, to illinois, and the panting
Chicago.
And then all ways, we go where flesh is cheap. Where factories

sit open, burning the chiefs. Make your way! Up through fog and
history
Make your way, and swing the general, that it come flash open

and spill the innards of that sweet thing we heard, and gave theory
to.
Breech, bridge, and reach, to where all talk is energy. And there's

enough, for anything singular. All our lean prophets and rhythms.
Entire
we arrive and set up shacks, hole cards, Western hearts at the edge

of saying. Thriving to balance the meanness of particular skies.
Race
of madmen and giants.

Brick songs. Shoe songs. Chants of open weariness.
Knife wiggle early evenings of the wet mouth. Tongue
dance midnight, any season shakes our house. Don't
tear my clothes! To doubt the balance of misery

ripping meat hug shuffle fuck. The Party of Insane
Hope. I've come from there too. Where the dead told lies
about clever social justice. Burning coffins voted
and staggered through cold white streets listening
to Willkie or Wallace or Dewey through the dead face
of Lincoln. Come from there, and belched it out.

I think about a time when I will be relaxed.
When flames and non-specific passion wear themselves
away. And my eyes and hands and mind can turn
and soften, and my songs will be softer
and lightly weight the air.

54 /

A POEM SOME PEOPLE WILL HAVE TO UNDERSTAND

Dull unwashed windows of eyes
and buildings of industry. What
industry do I practice? A slick
colored boy, 12 miles from his
home. I practice no industry.
I am no longer a credit
to my race. I read a little,
scratch against silence slow spring
afternoons.
    I had thought, before, some years ago
that I'd come to the end of my life.
    Watercolor ego. Without the preciseness
a violent man could propose.
    But the wheel, and the wheels,
wont let us alone. All the fantasy
    and justice, and dry charcoal winters
All the pitifully intelligent citizens
    I've forced myself to love.

  We have awaited the coming of a natural
  phenomenon. Mystics and romantics, knowledgeable
  workers
  of the land.

  But none has come.
  (Repeat)
    but none has come.

Will the machinegunners please step forward?

HOUDINI

Poured, white powder
on the back of a book
took out my plastic funnel
and honked the powder
up.

Then sit down, to write
before consciousness
drained away. Feeling
the change, the bag-like quality
of ease.

This will be
the last sense I make
for hours.

LETTER TO E. FRANKLIN FRAZIER

Those days when it was all right
to be a criminal, or die, a postman's son,
full of hallways and garbage, behind the hotdog store
or in the parking lots of the beautiful beer factory.

Those days I rose through the smoke of chilling Saturdays
hiding my eyes from the shine boys, my mouth and my flesh
from their sisters. I walked quickly and always alone
watching the cheap city like I thought it would swell
and explode, and only my crooked breath could put it together
again.

By the projects and small banks of my time. Counting my steps
on tar or new pavement, following the sun like a park. I imagined
a life, that was realer than speech, or the city's anonymous
fish markets. Shuddering at dusk, with a mile or so up the hill

to get home. Who did you love
then, Mussolini? What were you thinking,
Lady Day? A literal riddle of image
was me, and my smell was a continent
of familiar poetry. Walking the long way,
always the long way, and up the steep hill.

Those days like one drawn-out song, monotonously
promising. The quick step, the watchful march march,
All were leading here, to this room, where memory
stifles the present. And the future, my man, is long
time gone.

THE PEOPLE BURNING
May-Day! May-Day!
—Pilot talk

They now gonna make us shut up. Ease
thru windows in eight dollar hats
sharpening their pencils on match books. List
our errors and lies, stumbling over our souls
in the dark, for the sake of unnatural advantage.

They now gonna line you up, ask you about God. Nail
your answers on the wall, for the bowling alley owners
to decide. They now gonna pretend they flowers. Snake stalked
large named vegetables, who have, if nothing else,
the title: World's Vilest Living Things.

The Dusty Hearts of Texas, whose most honest world
is the long look into darkness, sensing the glittering
affront of reason or faith or learning. Preferring
fake tiger smells rubbed on the balls, and clothes
the peasants of no country on earth would ever be
vulgar enough to wear. The legacy of diseased mediocrity.

Become an Italian or Jew. Forget the hatred of natural
insolence. The teetering sense of right, as balance, each
natural man must have. Become a Jew, and join the union,
forget about Russia or any radicalism past a hooked grin.
Become an Italian quietist in some thin veneer of reasonable
gain. Lodi, Metuchen, Valley Stream, welcomes you into its
leather ridiculousness. Forget about any anarchy except the
understandable urge to be violent, or flashy, or fast, or
heavy fisted. Sing at Radio City, but never rage at the chosen,
for they have given you the keys to their hearts. Made you
the Fridays and Saturdays of the regime, clothed you in promise
and utility, and banned your thinkers to worship the rags
of your decline.

For the Reconstruction, for the march into any anonymous America,
stretches beyond hills of newsprint, and dishonorable intention.
Forget any dignity, but that that is easily purchased. And recognized
by Episcopalians as they pay their garbage bills. The blueprint's sound.

And the nation is smaller and the loudest mouths are recognized
and stunned by the filth of their hopeless truths. (I've got to
figure this all out. Got to remember just where I came in. Freedom Suite,
some five six years ago, Rollins cradling the sun, as it rose, and we
dreamed then, of becoming, unlike our fathers, and the other cowboys,
strong men in our time, raging and clawing, at fools of any persuasion.)

Now they ask me to be a jew or italian, and turn from the moment
disappearing into the shaking clock of treasonable safety, like reruns
of films, with sacred coon stars. To retreat, and replay; throw my mind out,
sit down and brood about the anachronistic God, they will tell you
is real. Sit down and forget it. Lean on your silence, breathing
the dark. Forget your whole life, pop your fingers in a closed room,
hopped-up witch doctor for the cowards of a recent generation. It is
choice, now, like a philosophy problem. It is choice, now, and
the weight is specific and personal. It is not an emotional decision.
There are facts, and who was it said, that this is a scientific century.

KENYATTA LISTENING TO MOZART

on the back trails, in sun glasses
and warm air blows cocaine from city
to river, and through the brains of
American poets in San Francisco.
                              Separate
              and lose. Spats brush through
                  undergrowths of fiction. Mathematics
              bird, undressed and in sympathy with absolute
                  stillness, and the neutrality of water. (We do not
      write poems in the rainy season.) Light to light,
    the weighted circumstance prowls like animals in the
bush.
    A zoo of consciousness,
                              cries and prowlings
anywhere. Stillness,
                  motion,
                         beings that fly, beings

that swim
exchanging
          in-
              formation.
                         Choice, and
                         style,
                                avail

and are beautiful
categories
                    If you go
                    for that.

THE NEW WORLD

The sun is folding, cars stall and rise
beyond the window. The workmen leave
the street to the bums and painters' wives
pushing their babies home. Those who realize
how fitful and indecent consciousness is
stare solemnly out on the emptying street.
The mourners and soft singers. The liars,
and seekers after ridiculous righteousness. All
my doubles, and friends, whose mistakes cannot
be duplicated by machines, and this is all of our
arrogance. Being broke or broken, dribbling
at the eyes. Wasted lyricists, and men
who have seen their dreams come true, only seconds
after they knew those dreams to be horrible conceits
and plastic fantasies of gesture and extension,
shoulders, hair and tongues distributing misinformation
about the nature of understanding. No one is that simple
or priggish, to be alone out of spite and grown strong
in its practice, mystics in two-pants suits. Our style,
and discipline, controlling the method of knowledge.
Beatniks, like Bohemians, go calmly out of style. And boys
are dying in Mexico, who did not get the word.
The lateness of their fabrication: mark their holes
with filthy needles. The lust of the world. This will not
be news. The simple damning lust,

                        float flat magic in low changing
                        evenings. Shiver your hands
                        in dance. Empty all of me for
                        knowing, and will the danger
                        of identification,

                Let me sit and go blind in my dreaming
                and be that dream in purpose and device.

                A fantasy of defeat, a strong strong man
                older, but no wiser than the defect of love.

HEGEL

Cut out
the insides,
where eyes
bungle their silence, and trains suffer
to be painted
by memory.
            This is turning. As a man
turns. Hardened or reconceived
sometimes the way we wish our lives
would be. "Let me do this
again,
      another way."

  Pushed to the wall
we fall away from each other
in this heresy. Dispute each other's
lives, as history. Or the common speech
of disaster, lacking a face or name, we give it
ours. And are destroyed by the very virtues
of our ignorance.
            I am not saying,
"Let the state fuck
its faggots,"
        only that no fag
        go unfucked, for purely impersonal
        reasons.

  I am trying to understand
the nightmare of economics. On the phone,
through the mails, I am afraid. I scream
for help. I scream
for help. And none comes, has ever
come. No single redeeming hand
has ever been offered,
           even against the excess
        of speech, no single redeeming
              word, has come
                  wringing out of flesh
            with the imperfect beautiful resolution

that would release me from this heavy contract
of emptiness.
          Either I am wrong
          or "he" is wrong. All right
          I am wrong, but give me someone
          to talk to.

LEADBELLY GIVES AN AUTOGRAPH

Pat your foot
and turn
           the corner. Nat Turner, dying wood
of the church. Our lot
is vacant. Bring the twisted myth
of speech. The boards brown and falling
away. The metal bannisters cheap
and rattly. Clean new Sundays. We thought
it possible to enter
the way of the strongest.

But it is rite that the world's ills
erupt as our own. Right that we take
our own specific look into the shapely
blood of the heart.
                    Looking thru trees
the wicker statues blowing softly against
the dusk.
Looking thru dusk
thru dark-
ness. A clearing of stars
and half-soft mud.

The possibilities of music. First
that it does exist. And that we do,
in that scripture of rhythms. The earth,
I mean the soil, as melody. The fit you need,
the throes. To pick it up and cut
away what does not singularly express.

Need.
Motive.
The delay of language.

A strength to be handled by giants.

The possibilities of statement. I am saying, now,
what my father could not remember
to say. What my grandfather

was killed
for believing.
        Pay me off, savages.
        Build me an equitable human assertion.

One that looks like a jungle, or one that looks like the cities
of the West.   But I provide the stock. The beasts
and myths.
        The City's Rise!
                (And what is history, then? **An old deaf lady**
                burned to death
                in South Carolina.

TONE POEM

(for Elvin Jones and Bob Thompson)

A host of loves is the city, and its memory
dead sense traveling (from England) on the sea
for two hundred years. The travelers show up in Japan
to promote peace and prosperity, perhaps a piece
of that nation's ass. Years later, years later,
plays rework the rime of lust. As history, and a cloud
their faces bang invisible notes, wind scribbled leaves
and foam. An eagle hangs above them spinning. Years and travelers
linger among the dead, no reports, gunshots white puffs
deciding the season and the mode of compromise. The general good
has no troops or armor, subtly the books stand closed, except
sad facts circled for unknown hippies carrying the mail.
I leave it there, for them, full of hope, and hurt. All the poems
are full of it. Shit and hope, and history. Read this line
young colored or white and know I felt the twist of dividing
memory. Blood spoiled in the air, caked and anonymous. Arms opening,
opened last night, we sat up howling and kissing. Men who loved
each other. Will that be understood? That we could, and still
move under cold nights with clenched fists. Swing these losers
by the tail. Got drunk then high, then sick, then quiet. But thinking
(and of you lovely shorties sit in libraries seeking such ideas out).
I'm here now, LeRoi, who tried to say something long for you. Keep it.
Forget me, or what I say, but not the tone, and exit image. No points,
or theories, from now on, just me and mine, when they get me, just
think of me as typing with a drink at my right hand, some women who
love me ... and the day growing old and sloppy through the window.

LOKU

Hold me she
told me I
did.

HISTORY AS PROCESS

1.

*The evaluation of the mysteries by the sons of all
experience.* All suffering, if we call the light a thing
all men should know. Or find. Where ever, in the dark folds
of the next second, there is some diminishing beauty we might one day
understand, and scream to, in some wild fit of acknowledged Godliness.

Reality, is what it is. This suffering truth
advertised in all men's loveliest histories.

The thing, There As Speed, is God, as mingling
possibility. The force. As simple future, what

the freaky gipsies rolled through Europe
on.

(The soul.)

2.

What can I do to myself? Bones
and dusty skin. Heavy eyes twisted
between the adequate thighs of all
humanity (a little h), strumming my head
for a living. Bankrupt utopia sez tell me
no utopias. I will not listen. (Except the raw wind
makes the hero's eyes close, and the tears that come out
are real.)

DAVID COPPERHEAD

On the stairs, in the house, on a street
in the world. Thought and wind, running.
Yellow clocks, Black wizards,
appear, and disappear, the woman I'm thinking
about is so beautiful. She controls my dreams,
and my reality. No choice, stirs a blue midnight
wind windy like cool brushes stuttering. The roof
is a stage, here all things go on. Go on.

(Booted twice, missed on the squeeze
and my arm shot up. A knot now, where
the high is wasted, and the head
only a little twittered, from
small heart, and lack of skill.)

Heart of a small dog, near water
in the summer. Winter, ice, and
slowness of the iron trees. What
have people to do with the world.
Whatever you think, the opposite
could also be. And any wavelength
in between.

(Now to consider, whether to go
again. I still need that feeling.
And sit robbed, my head twists,
from that lack. Always, and never,
a rationalist. But gut thought
rubbing all surfaces. Knife gripped hard
in the hand. Let fire break out
and stop us. Forget pink cardboard
suns. Gold halos. Slow run of water.
Some women are around. They walk and
never even miss us. He flies down
from the stage. The moon is gone.)

Feeling predicts
intelligence. The boats, pointing
West.

THE BRONZE BUCKAROO

for Herb Jeffries

Soft night comes back
with its clangs and dreams. Back
in through the base
of the hairy skull. The heavy pictures, unavailable
solaces, emptying their churchy magic
out. Golden girls, and thin black ones
patrol the dreamer's meat. Things
shovel themselves, from where they always are. Spinning, a
moment's indecision, past the vision of stealth and silence
Byron thought the night could be. Death blow Eliot silence, dwindling
away, in the 20th century. Poet clocks crouched in their Americas.
Dreaming of poems, only the cold sky could bring. Not room poems, or
fireplace poems, or the great washed poetry of our dizzy middleclass.
But something creeps and grabs them, rapes them on the pavement. The Screams
are not essays, rich blonde poetess from the mysteries of Kipling's harmon
nica! Not guileful treatises of waste and desire, stuck somewhere
nursing her tilted beauty, like some old fashion whore, embarrassed
by God, or his diseases. The funny heart blows smoke, in the winter
and gives us all the earth we need. In summer, it sweats, and remembers.
Half way up the hill the mutineers stand, and seek their comrades out.
I am half way up, and standing.

TARGET STUDY

NUMBERS, LETTERS

If you're not home, where
are you? Where'd you go? What
were you doing when gone? When
you come back, better make it good.
What was you doing down there, freakin' off
with white women, hangin' out
with Queens, say it straight to be
understood straight, put it flat and real
in the street where the sun comes and the
moon comes and the cold wind in winter
waters your eyes. Say what you mean, dig
it out put it down, and be strong
about it.

I cant say who I am
unless you agree I'm real

I cant be anything I'm not
Except these words pretend
to life not yet explained,
so here's some feeling for you
see how you like it, what it
reveals, and that's me.

Unless you agree I'm real
that I can feel
whatever beats hardest
at our black souls

I am real, and I can't say who
I am. Ask me if I know, I'll say
yes, I might say no. Still, ask.

I'm Everett LeRoi Jones, 30 yrs old.
A black nigger in the universe. A longer breath singer,
wouldbe dancer, strong from years of fantasy
and study. All this time then, for what's happening
now. All that spilling of white ether, clocks in ghostheads
lips drying and rewet, eyes opening and shut, mouths churning.

I am a meditative man. And when I say something it's all of me
saying, and all the things that make me, have formed me, colored me
this brilliant reddish night. I will say nothing that I feel is
lie, or unproven by the same ghostclocks, by the same riders
always move so fast with the word slung over their backs or
in saddlebags, charging down Chinese roads. I carry some words,
some feeling, some life in me. My heart is large as my mind
this is a messenger calling, over here, over here, open your eyes
and your ears and your souls; today is the history we must learn
to desire. There is no guilt in love

YOUNG SOUL

First, feel, then feel, then
read, or read, then feel, then
fall, or stand, where you
already are. Think
of your self, and the other
selves ... think
of your parents, your mothers
and sisters, your bentslick
father, then feel, or
fall, on your knees
if nothing else will move you,
                          then read
                          and look deeply
                          into all matters
                          come close to you
                          city boys—
                          country men

                          Make some muscle
                          in your head, but
                          use the muscle
                          in yr heart

CONFIRMATION

The blood in me, assumes a beautiful shape, it assumes
that I can write, and that I am the great mind of my own
soul, in a fit of fall flashing bells, the great booms
and machines that make the world worth exploding and re-
building, for whatever we agree on is most honorable.

There is no struggle to speak if you want to.
There is no slowness or stupidity we must bear.
There is perfection! There is grace! There are
all those things they talked about . . . but different!
Jesus Christ, how different! How much bullshit did they
put into our way, how much ugliness we canonized, dazed
and dazzing in
The Music is so strong,
it smashes through the boards. It questions
the beat of my mind, where the soul beats against the iron badges
of a cage. How hateful can be anything. How it can turn you, resur-
rect your errors as if the mind laughed at what it hated to use, and
used the fingers of your consciousness to dazzle yourself with madness.

We can be used by everything. We are not in danger of being wrong.
Only stupid, in the quiet despotic night. Oh, how the freaks of this
adventure sadden, the old ladies walking by scared and scaring, not
even caring that the world is falling apart, and even the intellectuals
will be killed. Oh, Christ you don't understand. I don't understand
what the problem has to do with this woman's lips, or that woman's
understanding of why is the world is finally so ugly, even though
you're right. The world is the most perfect thing in the soul. The world
is a soul, and we are souls if we remember the murmurs of the spirit.

FRIDAY

*And so we leave. Hurrying. The bags packed,
minds in halfzoom position. One kit I carry,
contents: 3 knives, a revolver, 1½ ounces of
bush. Then get in
the wind.*

All ready. All
right. Clinks jingles cries
through doors and windows
where the sun follows, in its quick breath,
matching our own I am rising. The air is still.
Heaven comics on the roof. My room sir william
butler will you answer the door of attention. To be
concerned, with ourselves, and the not knowing
even as the wind marauds, and the Gods change
faces.

When you are dead Good. And let the crying cease. Baroomed off a ship
where the ghosts of magic fucking conduct their pitiful search.

The social butterflies have turned to Pterodactyls. A poetic bird
of the second measure. The measure of the rhythm, hear me, stretching
past Your eyes.
    Oh simple weak minded gods,
   who walk the simple streets of circumstances. Who lie
  to people, to animals, to doors and excellent rugs. Oh power
 full juggernauts whose most powerful image is the hairy cock
 sucker of art. (Uncle Sam is a queer whose ass hangs open with
 the brown odor of his heroes' delight. Pimps whose mothers ate
 vermin from the chauffeur's piles, and giggled like the sweet babies of
 innocent adventure.) A fart over the world demanding the power of our
lives.
 Oh, later, later for them. Let them go out of our lives.
Let them kill themselves in their cars, or debowel themselves
with their useless energies.
      Even softer, come on, sit down now,
    relent. The window is open. Soft cars rise and
   fall. Your mind and eyes are open. You are strong. Leave
them Leave
them

/ 75

HERE HE COMES AGAIN

Dark crowds in my face, my lips
get big and important my nose
is suddenly strange mixture of
temperament and temperature. All
the black sealed in me flies to
the surface, and beneath it, more
of the same. Like a hard deep rock
I had to tell a hooknosed lady panting
at my fly, I didn't care whether she died
I had my own history of deaths and submission

I DON'T LOVE YOU

Whatever you've given me, whiteface glass
to look through, to find another there, another
what motherfucker? another bread tree mad at its
sacredness, and the law of some dingaling god, cold
as ice cucumbers, for the shouters and the wigglers,
and what was the world to the words of slick nigger fathers,
too depressed to explain why they could not appear to be men.

The bread fool. The don'ts of this white hell. The crashed eyes
of dead friends, standin at the bar, eyes focused on actual ugliness.

I don't love you. Who is to say what that will mean. I don't
love you, expressed the train, moves, and uptown days later
we look up and breathe much easier

I don't love you

WILL THEY CRY WHEN YOU'RE GONE, YOU BET

You leave dead friends in
a desert. But they've deserted
you, and them-
selves, and are leaving
themselves,
in the foot paths
of madmen and saints
enough sense to get away
from the dryness and uselessness
of such relaxation, dying in the dry
light, sand packed in their mouths
eyes burning, white women serenade them
in mystic deviousness, which is another
way of saying they're seeing things, which
are not really there, except for them,
never to find an oasis, even bitter water
which we get used to, is better than
white drifting fairies, muses, singing
to us, in calm tones, about how it is better to die
etcetera, than go off from them, how it is better to
lie in the cruel sun with your eyes turning to dunes
than leave them alone in that white heat,

WHAT AM I OFFERED

Six foot tall, once president
united states, small letters for
10 years, drawls, what they used
to call, Texas . . . cow-boy . . . talk,
scrawls, rolls, lies, all washed away
smoke rising over the moon, still red,
blood of the century twisting long drops
hung down through space,
                          can work as hustler
                          cracklicker, or brilliant god
                          (in a reconstructed devil world.

                          Strong beliefs, Hairless,
                          Very very white.

COLD TERM II

We make crazy lullabies
heartpushing, wailing in the innards
shit thrown across the blue heavens
spelling constant cool despair. Why
am I like this Knowing the world
so well yet open to its dumbest
disorders? I wanted a black woman.
And had one. She went away. I drove her
away, and had nothing left
but the endless mosquito babble
of my weakness. The Dancing Crimes
so full of wisdom we overlook the pure shit
involved. A landscape
made of
shit. A world.

SAD COWBOY

All the world, is hatred
and I think I am love, or where are you fool
to think you're different from some body,
you've felt pain, your mind has opend as meat
and sweat. The place, is the final determination.
What is your place in the order of your feelings?
As the runner for your nation, focused on their needs,
what can you say or dream or float wild copper love in place of,
what you had, which was white and soft, and the vision of the farm
boy, standing in his shit. Replacing the man, and defining his demise.
But that crap is finished. I move with the rest, as strong as they,
knowing my own mind to be the unneeded rationale, the kindly explanation.

BLUE WHITIE

Strange corpses the ones who
still talk. Here is one now.
Tell us, sir, why are you so
full of shit? Now, come on, Man, don't be afraid,
speak right up into the microphone.

PREMISES NOT QUITE CONDEMNED

An altered man
in the sea of a city
in his head he's a dreamer
white women and cars, the rotting artifacts
of lost uncivilizations. His hair is long,
his face round, sometimes soft voice smiles
toward the seat of desire.
                      What is the prediction
                      of the peoples? What is their pleasure?
                      Will they let him live who has sinned
                      for his strength through the garbage
                      of his ways? Will they let him breathe
                      in the maze he has created, riding
                      on his shoulders through the gale
                      of his invective. The children
                      of his thinking, are stronger
                      than he is, will they pity or
                      respect, the old old infant.

                Here's the drum that is his head
                and the scale that is his logic

                Rolled on the streets of the niggers.

Call him down
Make him talk

And an explanation start.

Let the old men have it
Let the punks take it

And let the strong men who he loves use him and his ways
for the strength of the peoples
and the strength of the logic
and his rest will be never, for the talk
he will inspire

Let him live, when he dies
and give birth to
brightness

RED EYE

(for Calvin Hernton and Ishmael Reed)

The corrupt madness of the individual. You cannot live
alone. You are in the world. World, fuck them. World rise
and twist like you do, night madness in rain as heavy as stones.
Alabama gypsy talk, for peeling lips. Look in your mother's head,
if you really want to know everything. Your sister's locked up
pussy. Invasion of the idea syndrome like hand clapping winter in.
Winter will make you move. Or you will freeze in Russia and
never live to see Napoleon as conceived by Marlon Brando.
We are at the point where death is too good for us. We are
in love with the virtue of evil. This communication. Rapping
on wet meat windows, they spin in your head, if I kill you
will not even have chance to hate me

LOWDOWN

We are in the era of imminent brake failure, breakdown
Country boys make believe they are emerging from pyramid crypts.
I talked to a man the other day, and he didn't want to say anything.
He just drove his train, dreaming of Columbia. Subway hollering roach children
to stretch the conductor out. Copper wire stretched to its maximum tolerance,
copper children loll in their chains dreaming of the chinese bomb. Now we
got the rhythm, and the first threat to White Eye since 1000 (Wogs slowed at
Tours, and the time got different. Era of The Man, now in decline, even
mailmen grow murderous offspring who sightsee in manhattan only to peep
closeup on suicide. The Wanderers. Time/Space syndrome, movement in space
as primitive as that is, as primitive as pimples in cold caves of Europe.
Red sores on their lips imagine what these men sought for the world. What
they wanted to give. For these long centuries. Their idealism was toejam.
Smeared on jewchrist, that's hunkie bread, turned green in the mold of
their shaky enterprises. Even paper not backed by gold. Last shot of three
different movies shows the money blown skyhigh to god, and other forces

WESTERN FRONT

My intentions are colors, I'm filled with
color, every tint you think of lends to mine
my mind is full of color, hard muscle streaks,
or soft glow round exactness registration. All earth
heaven things, hell things, in colors circulate
a wild blood train, turns litmus like a bible coat,
describes music falling flying, my criminal darkness,
static fingers, call it art, high above the streetwalkers
high above real meaning, floaters prop themselves in pillows
letting soft blondes lick them into serenity. Poems are made
by fools like Allen Ginsberg, who loves God, and went to India
only to see God, finding him walking barefoot in the street,
blood sickness and hysteria, yet only God touched this poet,
who has no use for the world. But only God, who is sole dope
manufacturer of the universe, and is responsible for ease
and logic. Only God, the baldhead faggot, is clearly responsible,
not, for definite, no cats we know.

20TH-CENTURY FOX

Dynamite black girl
fucking in the halls
skirt pulled up
climbing cross the walls

Dynamite black girl
in her dreams, in her motions, in her pull down hat,
sticks out her lip
asks me where I'm at

Dynamite black girl
outside the shaky mansions of whiteladies
she wears no gown dragging bonebodies of the starving,
nor is she grooved to be talked to by artistic chalksissyghosts

Dynamite black girl,
walks in the snow
meets me in the city
walks with me
stares at me
touches me
talks and talks
to me
kisses me
makes love,
        we said awhile back
        Dynamite black girl
        swingin' in the halls
        the world cant beat you
        and my slaps are love

POEM

For their clean bodies, and malcolm's eyes
I walk the streets confused and half sick
with despair at what I must do, yet the doing
as it's finally possible, drags me on. The way out
feeling inside where I reach, the stones and lights
of new town, new black, new strength, new wealth,
all come down, and back, and the length, of my
health.
My world
There's not a feeling or fissure sailing
to the stars. Not a strong lady dancing
on the heads of fat white guys, who lick
their bony lips or suck their gray fat teeth.
You see the men who die of cancer and heart trouble.
You see their niggers, fat men with freckles whose minds
are like endless garbage cans, full of blue rats and lies
and the stale vomit of dead Greeks. What is the soul to do
but expand. In the circle of being, the cycle of spirit, the closeness
of love when it's us who are loved, and made huge by some lady
we feel in our speech, or the image of home, in the valley of the blind,
we give them eyes, who we lost, where they drive the suitcases of
glassmenagerie widows, like it's illinois freaks popping their fingers
to Patti Page (who is for future reference, a dumb bitch), if the world
was the man or the god or the song of some specific dier, what more
could you say about it? Who are you walking through the night, where
is this night, my heart expands in the darkness, and sings, if it can,

We say, you will never
understand yourself as an object.
You don't know how you got here,
where you're going, so what's all this bullshit
philosophy

READING AND WEEPING

Lust hearts stalk nights
dreaming heroes of them
selves, lust
hearts, screaming
soul, soul, soul, soul,
without the least
memory
of what a soul is
like, they stalk
nights dreaming
reality is their
dying flesh, predicting
the deaths of everyone
but themselves, who are
already, dead, and fixed
to their deadness even
in warm spring wind.

Do not cross lust
hearts, they mean
to be killers, and
it is no matter that
you be black or sterilely
pale, they will kill you
if you cross them, if you
dare to speak of a breathing
world, they will menace you if
you are stronger than they are,
they will try to bring you down,
beware the lust hearts, you see them
slinking through the world certain of
their beauty, but look at them, and make them
look at themselves, it is a horrible experience.

POEM FOR RELIGIOUS FANATICS

There is a sickness to the black man
living in white town. Either he is white
or he hates white, but even in hating, he
reflects, the dead image of his surrounding.
His moon is saw dust marble. His walk is long
and fast, because he doesn't want the reality
of his impotence to sting, instead he will sting
you, before you ask him to look deeply into any reflector
and see himself eating gravel and dust, and old wood hearts.
There is a sickness to the black man in white town, because
he begins to believe he can beat everybody's ass, and he can,
down there, where each man is an island, and the heaviest bomber,
throwing down tnt can establish some conditional manhood in the land
of the dead, in the country of the blind. A one-eyed man, with rotting
palms, king of the tribes of the lost and the dead.

>   But we have gone away
>   from you, one-eyed man, cannibal,
>   o slickest weapon of the romes
>   we have left you, to come back
>   to ourselves. We have gone away from
>   the dead forests of your allergic kingdom
>   away from your evil fear of women, away from
>   your heavy screamings of anti-fact, and left you
>   with your brothers, who are no kin to you at all.

PRECISE TECHNIQUES

No immature bullshitting,
No threatening of people's lifes for bullshit objectives.
No more being a quick Nigger Hero.
The Tony Curtis of the Black Plague.
Because all that is white, no matter your bald
stares out on children playing on the sidewalk,
and pretend you would rule them with a selfish complex.
There is no dream of Man that haunts him such as Freedom!
Dispossessed spirits feeding on soulmeat. Because they do not know enough
to hate the white man, Or deal him those fancy death blows. God
is not a nigger with a beard. Nor
is he not. Question principles not
excitement. And what you laugh at will be hip
anyway

COLD TERM

All the things. The objects.
Cold freeze of the park, while
passing. People there. White inside
outside on horses trotting ignorantly
There is so much pain for our blackness
so much beauty there, if we think to what
our beautiful selves would make
of the world, steaming turning blackouts
over cold georgia, the spirits hover
waiting for the world to arrive at ecstasy.
Why cant we love each other and be beautiful?
Why do the beautiful corner each other and spit
poison? Why do the beautiful not hangout together
and learn to do away with evil? Why are the beautiful
not living together and feeling each other's trials?
Why are the beautiful not walking with their arms around
each other laughing softly at the soft laughter of black beauty?
Why are the beautiful dreading each other, and hiding from
each other? Why are the beautiful sick and divided
like myself?

JITTERBUGS

The imperfection of the world
is a burden, if you know it, think
about it, at all. Look up in the sky
wishing you were free, placed so terribly
in time, mind out among new stars, working
propositions, and not this planet where you
cant go anywhere without an awareness of the hurt
the white man has put on the people. Any people. You
cant escape, there's no where to go. They have made
this star unsafe, and this age, primitive, though yr mind
is somewhere else, your ass aint.

WORD FROM THE RIGHT WING

President Johnson
is a mass murderer,
and his mother,
was a mass murderer,
and his wife
is weird looking, a special breed
of hawkbill cracker
and his grandmother's
weird dumb and dead
turning in the red earth
sick as dry blown soil
and he probably steals
hates magic
and has no use
for change, tho changing, and changed
the weather plays its gambling
tune. His mother is a dead blue cloud.
He has negroes work for him hate him,
wish him under the bullets of kennedydeath
OPEN FIRE FROM THE SCHOOL WINDOWS
these projectiles kill his mother plagued
by vulgar cancer, floating her dusty horoscope,
without the love even she thinks she needs, deadbitch,
Johnson's mother, walked all night holding hands
with a nigger, and stroked that nigger's
hard. Blew him downtown Newark 1928 . . . I got proof

NEWSHIT

1.

The lovers speak to each other as if they were born
this second without anything but the world and their vision
which is a blue image of themselves, on 7th ave drinking, and
pretending to be the few things of value in the world.

We all need to tighten up. We all need each other. We all
need to stop lying and lock arms and look at each other
like black humans struggling with depraved eagles.

But the part of the whole that does not insist on its wholeness.
The dark, the shadow, the wealth of all our lives. Where is this
stored? And who is the master who corrupts the silence of our
beautiful consciousness.

2.

The heart
is love, is the soul, stretched out dying
they killed him he's dying stretched out cars
trampling his papers. An old dead man, wanted
life, killed in the street, screams, for light.

LIGHT LIGHT LIGHT LIGHT LIGHT LIGHT LIGHT LIGHT

he screams as if the world were a cellar, and nothing
in it reflected his needs.

        I am a mad nigger in love with everything
        You make it impossible to be myself in this
        place. Where can I go? Where is my self to
        live in this shaky universe.

        Oh love in the women of the world. Oh heart
        in the dungeon of the earth. Oh people who
        love me for being alive, help me, the world
        is changing, and I change, forever, with it.

SONG

I love you
love me
let's get together
& go to
sea
& stay
away
& fuck
all day
    please miss blackie
    can we split
    I'll kiss
    your mouth
    pull yr tit.
        Gently
        as sun
        as breeze
        where we go
        please
        miss
        blackie
        can we blow?

LADY BUG

The motherfuckin'
heart, of the
motherfuckin'
day, grows hot
as a bitch, on her
motherfuckin'
way, back home.

I want to go
back home.

I've got nothin'
against you. But I
got to get
back home.

THREE MOVEMENTS AND A CODA

THE QUALITY OF NIGHT THAT YOU HATE MOST IS ITS BLACK
AND ITS STARTEETH EYES, AND STICKS ITS STICKY FINGERS
IN YOUR EARS, RED NIGGER EYES LOOKING UP FROM A BLACK HOLE.
RED NIGGER LIPS TURNING KILLER GEOMETRY, LIKE HIS EYES ROLL UP
LIKE HE THOUGHT RELIGION WAS BEBOP

                      LIKE HE THOUGHT RELIGION WAS
                      REBOP ... SIXTEEN KILLERS ON A
                      LIVE MAN'S CHEST ...
                                    THE LONE RANGER

IS DEAD
THE SHADOW
IS DEAD.
ALL YOUR HEROES ARE DYING. J. EDGAR HOOVER WILL
SOON BE DEAD. YOUR MOTHER WILL DIE. LYNDON JOHNSON,

                                          these are natural
                                          things. No one is
                                          threatening anybody
                                          thats just the way life
                                          is,
                                          boss.

Red Spick talking to you from a foxhole very close to the
Vampire Nazis' lines. I can see a few Vampire Nazis moving very quickly
back and forth under the heavy smoke. I hear, and perhaps you do, in
the back ground, the steady deadly cough of mortars, and the light shatter
of machine guns.

BANZAI!! BANZAI!! BANZAI!! BANZAI!!

Came running out of the drugstore window with
an electric alarm clock, and then dropped the motherfucker
and broke it. Go get somethin' else. Take everything in there.
Look in the cash register. TAKE THE MONEY. TAKE THE MONEY. YEH.
TAKE IT ALL. YOU DONT HAVE TO CLOSE THE DRAWER. COME ON MAN, I SAW
A TAPE RECORDER BACK THERE.

    These are the words of lovers
    Of dancers, of dynamite singers
    These are songs if you have the
      music

T. T. JACKSON SINGS

I fucked your mother
on top of a house
when I got through
she thought she was
Mickey Mouse.

I fucked your mother
under a tree
when it was over
she couldn't even pee

I fucked your mother
and she hollered OOOO
she thought I was
fu man chu

I fucked your mother
and she started to grin
then she found out
it wasn't even in.

RETURN OF THE NATIVE

Harlem is vicious
modernism. BangClash.
Vicious the way its made.
Can you stand such beauty?
So violent and transforming.
The trees blink naked, being
so few. The women stare
and are in love with them
selves. The sky sits awake
over us. Screaming
at us. No rain.
Sun, hot cleaning sun
drives us under it.

The place, and place
meant of
black people. Their heavy Egypt.
(Weird word!) Their minds, mine,
the black hope mine. In Time.
We slide along in pain or too
happy. So much love
for us. All over, so much of
what we need. Can you sing
yourself, your life, your place
on the warm planet earth.
And look at the stones

the hearts, the gentle hum
of meaning. Each thing, life
we have, or love, is meant
for us in a world like this.
Where we may see ourselves
all the time. And suffer
in joy, that our lives
are so familiar.

GOODBYE!

                If we call
                to ourselves
                if we want to feel
                who we are if
                we want to love
                what we can
                be
                come
                into
                a wide space
                of heart
                and hearts
                meaning
                we love (love love
(these are soft cries of feeling
can you help me, who are here w/me can
you walk into my deep senses

I want you to understand the world
as I have come to understand it
I'll wait here a few seconds, please come

BLACK BOURGEOISIE,

        has a gold tooth, sits long hours
        on a stool thinking about money.
        sees white skin in a secret room
        rummages his sense for sense
        dreams about Lincoln (s)
        conks his daughter's hair
        sends his coon to school
        works very hard
        grins politely in restaurants
        has a good word to say
        never says it
        does not hate ofays
        hates, instead, him self
        him black self

A POEM FOR BLACK HEARTS

For Malcolm's eyes, when they broke
the face of some dumb white man, For
Malcolm's hands raised to bless us
all black and strong in his image
of ourselves, For Malcolm's words
fire darts, the victor's tireless
thrusts, words hung above the world
change as it may, he said it, and
for this he was killed, for saying,
and feeling, and being/change, all
collected hot in his heart, For Malcolm's
heart, raising us above our filthy cities,
for his stride, and his beat, and his address
to the gray monsters of the world, For Malcolm's
pleas for your dignity, black men, for your life,
black man, for the filling of your minds
with righteousness, For all of him dead and
gone and vanished from us, and all of him which
clings to our speech black god of our time.
For all of him, and all of yourself, look up,
black man, quit stuttering and shuffling, look up,
black man, quit whining and stooping, for all of him,
For Great Malcolm a prince of the earth, let nothing in us rest
until we avenge ourselves for his death, stupid animals
that killed him, let us never breathe a pure breath if
we fail and white men call us faggots till the end of
the earth.

BLACK ART

SOS

Calling black people
Calling all black people, man woman child
Wherever you are, calling you, urgent, come in
Black People, come in, wherever you are, urgent, calling
you, calling all black people
calling all black people, come in, black people, come
on in.

BLACK ART

Poems are bullshit unless they are
teeth or trees or lemons piled
on a step. Or black ladies dying
of men leaving nickel hearts
beating them down. Fuck poems
and they are useful, wd they shoot
come at you, love what you are,
breathe like wrestlers, or shudder
strangely after pissing. We want live
words of the hip world live flesh &
coursing blood. Hearts Brains
Souls splintering fire. We want poems
like fists beating niggers out of Jocks
or dagger poems in the slimy bellies
of the owner-jews. Black poems to
smear on girdlemamma mulatto bitches
whose brains are red jelly stuck
between 'lizabeth taylor's toes. Stinking
Whores! We want "poems that kill."
Assassin poems, Poems that shoot
guns. Poems that wrestle cops into alleys
and take their weapons leaving them dead
with tongues pulled out and sent to Ireland. Knockoff
poems for dope selling wops or slick halfwhite
politicians Airplane poems, rrrrrrrrrrrrrrrr
rrrrrrrrrrrrrrr . . . tuhtuhtuhtuhtuhtuhtuhtuh
. . . rrrrrrrrrrrrrrrr . . . Setting fire and death to
whities ass. Look at the Liberal
Spokesman for the jews clutch his throat
& puke himself into eternity . . . rrrrrrrr
There's a negroleader pinned to
a bar stool in Sardi's eyeballs melting
in hot flame Another negroleader
on the steps of the white house one
kneeling between the sheriff's thighs
negotiating coolly for his people.
Agggh . . . stumbles across the room . . .
Put it on him, poem. Strip him naked
to the world! Another bad poem cracking
steel knuckles in a jewlady's mouth

Poem scream poison gas on beasts in green berets
Clean out the world for virtue and love,
Let there be no love poems written
until love can exist freely and
cleanly. Let Black People understand
that they are the lovers and the sons
of lovers and warriors and sons
of warriors Are poems & poets &
all the loveliness here in the world

We want a black poem. And a
Black World.
Let the world be a Black Poem
And Let All Black People Speak This Poem
Silently
or LOUD

FOR A LADY I KNOW.

Talk the talk I need
you, as you resurrect
your consciousness above
the streets, as you walk
with me, and lay
with me, and wonder
what is on
my mind. Oh talk, talk,
lady, and remind yrself
that you are dealing
with a spirit, deal, madam,
in your bigassed smiling eyes
in the world of real things—
as I have pronounced the life
in our fingers, real, so you must be
and grow to love me, as I must, of
course, finally, fall on my knees,
with love for you.

POEM FOR HALFWHITE COLLEGE STUDENTS

Who are you, listening to me, who are you
listening to yourself? Are you white or
black, or does that have anything to do
with it? Can you pop your fingers to no
music, except those wild monkies go on
in your head, can you jerk, to no melody,
except finger poppers get it together
when you turn from starchecking to checking
yourself. How do you sound, your words, are they
yours? The ghost you see in the mirror, is it really
you, can you swear you are not an imitation grayboy,
can you look right next to you in that chair, and swear,
that the sister you have your hand on is not really
so full of Elizabeth Taylor, Richard Burton is
coming out of her ears. You may even have to be Richard
with a white shirt and face, and four million negroes
think you cute, you may have to be Elizabeth Taylor, old lady,
if you want to sit up in your crazy spot dreaming about dresses,
and the sway of certain porters' hips. Check yourself, learn who it is
speaking, when you make some ultrasophisticated point, check yourself,
when you find yourself gesturing like Steve McQueen, check it out, ask
in your black heart who it is you are, and is that image black or white,

you might be surprised right out the window, whistling dixie on the way in.

A SCHOOL OF PRAYER

      A hollow eye sees moons dance
music in the pupil as it studies the changing
 world, We are all beautiful (except white
people, they are full of, and made of
 shit) O black people full of illusions
and weird power. O my loves and my heart
 pumping black blood screaming through
my thickened veins

        Do not obey their laws
        which we are against God
        believe brother, do not
        ever think any of that
        cold shit they say is
        true. They are against
        the law. Their "laws"
        are filthy evil, against
        almighty God. They are
        sick to be against God,
        against the animals and sun,
        against thought and feeling
        against the world as it most commonly
        is. That is they are against
        beauty. Do not let them show you
        a beer can, except believe their profundity
        is as easily read. Do not believe or shelter them.
        Do not let them eat your children. Do not believe
        or shelter them, or shelter their slickbullshit
        for one second in your heart.

The eye sees. The I. The self. Which passes out and into
the wind. We are so beautiful we talk at the same time
and our breathing is harnessed to divinity.

BIOGRAPHY

Hangs.
whipped
blood
striped
meat pulled
clothes ripped
slobber
feet dangled
pointing
noised
noise
churns
face
black sky
and moon
leather night
red
bleeds
drips
ground
sucks
blood
hangs
life wetting
sticky
mud

laughs
bonnets
wolfmoon
crazyteeth

hangs

hangs
granddaddy
granddaddy, they tore

his
neck

RED LIGHT

The only thing we know is the thing
we turn out to be, I don't care what
you think, its true, now you think
your way out of this

LITTLE BROWN JUG

Who are you?
A lost brother.
A singer. A song
I lost, almost, sat up
one night, itched
till it came
to me, cried
one night, happy
that it played
through me.

Little Brown Jug. Nigger Brother.
Dust singer in
the shadow of old
fences. Companion, of melody
rhythm
turned around heart runs
climbed & jumped screaming
WE ARE GODS, as we
sailed years through the firmament
landing beside a
garage, Dear brother, song
slides the streets, circles the cold,
sweats on summer fruit, Oh I
love my black energy &
lost brother father serenade
me, as world-solo, the spirits
bubble, loft, & say
where you are. I suffer
to hear you so tough
& know all the spooks
who need to.

W.W.

Back home the black women are all beautiful,
and the white ones fall back, cutoff from 1000
years stacked booty, and Charles of the Ritz
where jooshladies turn into billy burke in blueglass
kicks. With wings, and jingly bew-teeful things.
The black women in Newark are fine. Even with all that grease
in their heads. I mean even the ones where the wigs
slide around, and they coming at you 75 degrees off course.
I could talk to them. Bring them around. To something.
Some kind of quick course, on the sidewalk, like Hey baby
why don't you take that thing off yo' haid. You look like
Miss Muffett in a runaway ugly machine. I mean. Like that.

CIVIL RIGHTS POEM

Roywilkins is an eternal faggot
His spirit is a faggot
his projection
and image, this is
to say, that if i ever see roywilkins
on the sidewalks
imonna
stick half my sandal
up his
ass

THE DEADLY EYES
ARE STARS!

        fools
        say, i've sd it

        and come to regret the white filth
        jamming thru my veins, come to hate

        the quiet well disposed "beauties" of the
        word, without substance, even opposed
        to it, as black hearts pumping through eyes

        cannot see stars, cannot see skies, cannot see
        anything, except the truth, the fat bulging lunatic

        eyes, of the white man, which are not stars, and his
        face, not sky, and him self, no God, just another lame

        in love with him self, at everybody else's expense. Why dont

        Somebody kill the motherfucker? Why dont somebody jam his head
        in his own shit? Why are all you chumps standing around

        doing nothing? Letting this creep tapdance on your dreams.

KA 'BA

A closed window looks down
on a dirty courtyard, and black people
call across or scream across or walk across
defying physics in the stream of their will

Our world is full of sound
Our world is more lovely than anyone's
tho we suffer, and kill each other
and sometimes fail to walk the air

We are beautiful people
with african imaginations
full of masks and dances and swelling chants
with african eyes, and noses, and arms,
though we sprawl in gray chains in a place
full of winters, when what we want is sun.

We have been captured,
brothers. And we labor
to make our getaway, into
the ancient image, into a new

correspondence with ourselves
and our black family. We need magic
now we need the spells, to raise up
return, destroy, and create. What will be

the sacred words?

BEAUTIFUL BLACK WOMEN ...

Beautiful black women, fail, they act. Stop them, raining.
They are so beautiful, we want them with us. Stop them, raining.
Beautiful, stop raining, they fail. We fail them and their lips
stick out perpetually, at our weakness. Raining. Stop them. Black
queens, Ruby Dee weeps at the window, raining, being lost in her
life, being what we all will be, sentimental bitter frustrated
deprived of her fullest light. Beautiful black women, it is
still raining in this terrible land. We need you. We flex our
muscles, turn to stare at our tormentor, we need you. Raining.
We need you, reigning, black queen. This/terrible black ladies
wander, Ruby Dee weeps, the window, raining, she calls, and her voice
is left to hurt us slowly. It hangs against the same wet glass, her
sadness and age, and the trip, and the lost heat, and the gray cold
buildings of our entrapment. Ladies. Women. We need you. We are still
trapped and weak, but we build and grow heavy with our knowledge. Women.
Come to us. Help us get back what was always ours. Help us. women. Where
are you, women, where, and who, and where, and who, and will you help
us, will you open your bodysouls, will you lift me up mother, will you
let me help you, daughter, wife/lover, will you

BABYLON REVISITED

The gaunt thing
with no organs
creeps along the streets
of Europe, she will
commute, in her feathered bat stomach-gown
with no organs
with sores on her insides
even her head
a vast puschamber
of pus (sy) memories
with no organs
nothing to make babies
she will be the great witch of euro-american legend
who sucked the life
from some unknown nigger
whose name will be known
but whose substance will not ever
not even by him
who is dead in a pile of dopeskin

This bitch killed a friend of mine named BobThompson
a black painter, a giant, once, she reduced
to a pitiful imitation faggot
full of American holes and a monkey on his back
slapped airplanes
from the empire state building

May this bitch and her sisters, all of them,
receive my words
in all their orifices like lye mixed with
cocola and alaga syrup

feel this shit, bitches, feel it, now laugh your
hysterectic laughs
while your flesh burns
and your eyes peel to red mud

MADNESS

                        The white man

at best

is

corny

but who is to say it how is the
who how is the black man? to say
what when he sits biting his ass
in the sun, or laid cross a puddle
for snailtitty to cross over, how
and with what logic and moral who
is fed by the meanest of streams
will we move, or will we be merely
proud, as the best, yet with will
to be ego, or self same mean bastards
corrupting our inch of despair. To try,
what, for what, who will appreciate, who
will benefit, to desert is no different or better,
they all have deserted and sit in the sun under a sign
spirits waving through summer and fall spirits in the cold
place of our crucifixion, break the man-head off the sign
it is a cross, a double dirty cross, to hang your civilization

what can we say, open your mouth
do your lips, read, look
why I want to confront you
why you are a child or dead old man
how can i move when they will not move with me
is this the dark room
is this the closed door
the empty face
the vanished strength

just big mouf niggers alright just big floats
alligator heads in the mardi gras, dance and cry
shadows of living deadmen, dance and cry
sit up scream in church, under the blinking sign
of the times, a bar, a pignostril parlor

proud of what
of what what tell me yeh tell me motherfucker
what are you proud, any of you. tell me, what
for being slaves, for dying, for watching them feeling them
chop you up vomit you out lie to you kill burn tear your eyes
out and your ears, with your soul string dangled under the
same cold sun, your soul string, which suffered and you left
and dont care, to be cool with tony bennett, an old nigger man
for you now, and the cars, for you now, or the slow pause of death,
for you junky whore red head fag twist bump jam caress the image
of stupidness, fried haid skinny bitch laughing at god, and "i'd
don't know," har har har, with pigs to give her chilrun, and
nothing but heartache since they ain't too proud to beg

for what even you long bushhead with the little glasses
a style of yr own to carry the futility more righteously
but no matter, the same criss cross ugly jealousy and white
vomit sometimes for brains. we poets drummers hornplayers, nationalists
running our corny shit on a people standin in the sun
rotting rotting for centuries destined to die with the
white man destined to die with the white man destined
to die with the white man, the white man we say we hate
the white man we want to kill the whiteman who kills us
the white man, WHO AT BEST IS VERY VERY CORNY DUDE
to we die you will at the best to very die destined falling
ground-face hands burned in the windows fall corny die
the legend will be
the suffering and sacrifice will be
gone
lost
done
never
no one will remember
except the lost servants died with their masters
when the rest of the spiritual world got fullup
with corniness and death
the eternal life
we know we are
lostdie
heart fall
up, "i'm hurt, help me, no stay with me nigger,

die with me nigger
look jump off the building
with me, nigger, jump jump
look how we fall through space, nigger,
sign you up to play at newport
you can run the jazzmobile
you want to go to lincoln center
look i'll give you the goddam academy award
letme slap your face dianne, let me, die with you, off the
building, falling, hurt, gone
lost
done
never
no one will remember
Hi Yo Silver .. Away!! we die with the white man
the buildings stick us in the heart
we die
with
oh no
please
not
not that
not with
oh please
can we
oh
not
lost
yest-
a ha,
a ha, ha, ha
a ha, ha, ha, ha, ha, ha, ha, hahahahahahahahahahahaha

kyrie kyrie kyrie elision

BLUDOO BABY WANT MONEY AND ALLIGATOR GOT IT TO GIVE

say day lay day may fay come some bum'll
take break jake make fake lay day some bum'll
say day came break snow mo whores red said they'd
lay day in my in fay bed to make bread for jake
limpin in the hall with quiverin stick
he's hiney raised, in a car by the curb,
licking his yellow lips, yellow snow yellow bubs
yellow eyes lookin at the dark, hears his whisper
says, "come down goily i give you a stick ... da da da
      come down goily i give you a pinch ... da da da
      come down goily i sit in my car ... da da da
      come down goily to where we gray guys are ... da da da ...
                                        da da da ...
                                        da da da ...
                                        da da da ..."

she's not thinkna him, seein him, seen people like him
dazed out there, suckin heavy vapors, her butt throw off,
like stick-it-in nitetime, for the dough, chile, for the money
baby, look at him down there, lookn up at me ... da da da
she and jake
look

da cuppd flame
fat claws, motor batting
outside miss workamo's house.

shd she go down she's pulling the coat
gainst the wind, will she let him, ol good guy
get in.
for the dough
mr tom
for your woman
in the mirror

shakin like a storm
psst oh miss, oh miss, oh oh, yellow, vapor butt got him
hung out the window
look down

jake jr.
and mr roy
there, look kin you help . . . da da da
kin you give me
somethin
can you make me
beautiful
with your bullshit
can you
love me
nigger
she askin us, jake jr
sis betty, where we at, at the pin of the stare, curld flag of misery,

oh the hip walk on that chile
fat sister, swashing that heavy ass
psst psst
oh miss miss,

yellow
cloud it up
stick it in
and jab down
under the wheel . . . da da da

miss
oh miss

stumbling down the stairs
when she turns to go back
and stick her head in the car
the motor's running, she already know the money's in her
slide

we throwin rocks and garbage cans
barry draggn the motherfucker out
stomp
bompa dee dee da, and run your heaviest
game,
baby, baby, take
it take it,

run on way,

baby, baby, take it
take it, baby

run on way,

money on the ground

blood on the ground

the first step

we protects
provides

the example
plain

when the sun
come up

again

STIRLING STREET SEPTEMBER

                                        (for Sylvia)

I CAN BE THE BEAUTIFUL BLACK MAN
because I am
the beautiful black man, and you, girl, child nightlove,
you are beautiful
too.
We are something, the two of us
the people love us for being
though they may call us out our
name, they love our strength
in the midst of, quiet, at the peak of,
violence, for the sake of, at the lust of
pure life, WE WORSHIP THE SUN,

We are strange in a way because we know
who we are. Black beings passing through
a tortured passage of flesh.

COPS

flyolfloyd, i know from barringer,
he used to be the daredevil sax playing
lover of the old sod, near the hip park
where they threw you in, he, with some others,
notably Allen Polite, was a lover, and smooth as anything blowin
in them parts, in that town, in that time
he weighs 400 now
and threatens junkies
on Howard Street, calling them by first or nick
names, really scaring the piss out of them, being
"a nice guy" and all his killings being accidental.
Bowleg Otis played football but was always a prick
he made detective by arresting a dude he knew all his life,
he waited in the cold counting white folks' smiles. Lenny
drives a panel truck, Leon parkd in front of the city hospital
bullshitting, but he'd split yr head. He was a bad catchr w/
Baxter Terrace, you slide home head first you get messed up
strong as a bitch. Hubert Friday, beat up Barry one night,
Hubie was a funnytime cat never played anything. Cats used to
pop his sister. You wanna stand in front of a bar, with a gun
pointed at you? You wanna try to remember why you liked somebody
while the bullet comes. Shit.

THE WORLD IS FULL OF REMARKABLE THINGS

(for little Bumi)

Quick Night
easy warmth
The girlmother lies next to me
breathing
coughing
sighing
at my absence. Bird Plane
Flying near Mecca
Sun sight warm air
through
my air foils. Womanchild
turns
lays her head
on my
stomach. Night aches
acts
Niggers rage

down the street. (Air
Pocket, sinks
us. She lady
angel brings
her self
to touch me
grains & grass & long
silences, the dark
ness my natural
element, in
warm black skin
I love &
understand
things. Sails
cries these
moans, pushed
from her by my
weight, her legs
spreading wrapping
secure the spirit
in her.

             We begin our
ritual breathing
flex the soul clean
out, her eyes slide
into   dreams

FROM THE EGYPTIAN

I will slaughter
the enemies
of my father
I will slay those
who have blinded
him.

I will slaughter
the
enemies
of ym
father
I will slay those
who have
blinded
him

To blind int race the slur tore slaw tearing
the eyes, ice cold broatish maggots babble-tering
battering the ice
kaltenborn machine gunned
avie's ave livingston presumed
trapped, sapped, capped by the living
nigger, traits for the traitorous nigger doctors
whose asses and stomachs cost more than telephones

cripple pipple
mine but cripple babbar
ooni
mc-rout and death cruel murder
rip their uniforms off and stomp feet in their throat
smash them, rip their bellies, bash the heads with stoned
niggers sailing across the world, broome street squadron
parked near West Kinney, when the light changes they leap
at the cars, the troats, yelling, tho, burd ies eyes tap
squish under mad tree crus crunch-oo good, my eyes, my baby
the face, george, oh god, please i didn't i didn't the nigger
cop bop stamp, his gun, fuck you, shit, AEEEERRRRRR, twist
blues hill rope yall mixd uuuh, ummuuua. the. ouaff. We. Ow
god, that woman i we were i the egyptian bar, looked at her,
the huge art object of destruction

Great thing
Great great thing
   great thing
        GREAAAAT
                Gre-e(a)t thing great thing great great thing
dirty fucking shit HEYAIEEE great scraping fuckin head yes diggair
dutair moto'freaking scrashteemash
                    car bashed into house fat legs
               upside down, and smashed bloody JESUS
           what'll we do, lets geh-uh ohh ra-ze ra-ze
              I will slaughter the enemies of my father
              I will slay those who have blinded him.

ELECTION DAY

The lies of young boys are to be heard about, or read about, or perhaps
generally tolerated, but the lies of an old man. Of a man growing bald
and fat. These are the lies of death. And the cloak of death they spread.
We can die from them. Like choked by underbrush, heavy weeds. We see him.
Pull the election lever, and men die in Graystone, electrocuted, or are
beat to death on the corners of dirty cities. By heroes. These are the
killers' heroes. Wd that they were our own.   And not the mad races killing
us. We have a nigger in a cape and cloak. Flying above the shacks and whores.
he has just won an election. A wop is his godfather. Praise Wop from whom
all blessing flow. The nigger edges sidewise in the light breeze, his fingers
scraping nervously in his palms. He has had visions. With commercials. Change
rattles in his pockets. He is high up. Look, he signals. Turns, backup, for
cheers. He swoops. The Wop is waving. Wave Wop. He swoops, he has a metal
mother-sister, loves him, made him from scrap iron. Taught him to fly. Wave
Metal sister. Grump and waddle. Grouch at heaven, love and God. Metal woman
wave the nigger in. He sails. Wopwaves. Crowds of neckless italians whistle
and tell jokes. Leaving rings around the East River. They swim with the goods.
"Hello, this is Heroin Plant Sardinia, How many bags you want Jefe?"
He is leading us, through the phonecalls and shootups. He is flying ahead,
giving being losing a head. I love him. He is made of iron and is steered
by a huge white joint. Fly councilman. He loves us. We are his people.
Look
he waves and sails. Tho the breeze is wind is gale and stiff and turns him
back and up against his will. Wave will. And sister ironhole. And neckless
ton of wop. Wave. Look. He loves and beckons to us. He is proceeded far
ahead, in purple fading rheumatic wings, by the aluminum coon. Long dead,
but pushed in the same heavy storm. His dry fly wings batting sideways
useless, lips eyes fingers squeezing shut and open wings flaking loose
in the wind. He is the old leader killed from booze and electricity. He is
The Flag, and turns his votes into pizzerias. The "new man" has a guideline
leads from alum to him, from ass to nose, and through the spine, and tied
with chains to the white quivering dick shoved halfway up his ass, its tip
like an enormous fishmouth is the victorious candidate's tongue. Talk vic
torious candidate, when you land, or while you fly. Talk, and wave. We moving
now. We see all of you hovering above us, gods of the unflushed commode.

Victorious candidate, we are your lowly slovenly ignorant people, and we
need no help. We are merely the scorekeepers for your hip enterprises. Oh,
victorious roundshouldered nigger candidate
daughter of a victorious roundshouldered nigger

mother-father. We are no
bodies. We are no merit.
We are to be used and killed
and lied to. Don't mind us, oh
victorious roundshouldered imitation
whiteman, fly on in your vacuum packed commode, do not fear us, we are
garbage, we are filth, listen to our dirty mouths, look at our loud
clothes and bad grammar. We are indeed scum, yr honor, lock us up.
We aint shit, baby. We aint nothin. Don't mind us, partner, jus go on head,
where you gon' go. All we can do is watch, That's all my man, just watch,
and maybe pray

LEROY

I wanted to know my mother when she sat
looking sad across the campus in the late 20's
into the future of the soul, there were black angels
straining above her head, carrying life from our ancestors,
and knowledge, and the strong nigger feeling. She sat
(in that photo in the yearbook I showed Vashti) getting into
new blues, from the old ones, the trips and passions
showered on her by her own. Hypnotizing me, from so far
ago, from that vantage of knowledge passed on to her passed on
to me and all the other black people of our time.
When I die, the consciousness I carry I will to
black people. May they pick me apart and take the
useful parts, the sweet meet of my feelings. And leave
the bitter bullshit rotten white parts
alone.

BLACK PEOPLE!

                What about that bad short you saw last week
on Frelinghuysen, or those stoves and refrigerators, record players
in Sears, Bambergers, Klein's, Hahnes', Chase, and the smaller joosh
enterprises? What about that bad jewelry, on Washington Street, and
those couple of shops on Springfield? You know how to get it, you can
get it, no money down, no money never, money dont grow on trees no
way, only whitey's got it, makes it with a machine, to control you
you cant steal nothin from a white man, he already stole it he owes
you anything you want, even his life. All the stores will open if you
will say the magic words. The magic words are: Up against the wall mother
fucker this is a stick up! Or: Smash the window at night (these are magic
actions) smash the windows daytime, anytime, together, let's smash the
window drag the shit from in there. No money down. No time to pay. Just
take what you want. The magic dance in the street. Run up and down Broad
Street niggers, take the shit you want. Take their lives if need be, but
get what you want what you need. Dance up and down the streets, turn all
the music up, run through the streets with music, beautiful radios on
Market Street,. they are brought here especially for you. Our brothers
are moving all over, smashing at jellywhite faces. We must make our own
World, man, our own world, and we cannot do this unless the white man
is dead. Let's get together and kill him my man, let's get to gather the fruit
of the sun, let's make a world we want black children to grow and learn in
do not let your children when they grow look in your face and curse you by
pitying your tomish ways.

TENZI
YA
IMAMU

CENSUS

BLACK PEOPLE BLACK PEOPLE BLACK PEOPLE BLACK PEOPLE BLACK PEOPLE
YELLOW PEOPLE YELLOW PEOPLE YELLOW PEOPLE YELLOW PEOPLE YELLOW PEOPLE
BROWN PEOPLE BROWN PEOPLE BROWN PEOPLE BROWN PEOPLE BROWN PEOPLE
RED PEOPLE RED PEOPLE RED PEOPLE RED PEOPLE RED PEOPLE
POOR PEOPLE POOR PEOPLE POOR PEOPLE POOR PEOPLE POOR PEOPLE POOR PEOPLE POOR PEOPLE POOR PEOPLE

. . . .
& others.

WIG POEM

take off the wig
take off the wig
take off the wig
take off the wig
take off the wig
take off the wig
take off the wig
take off the wig
take off the wig

CHILD EVOLVE

Bobby, Stanley, JB, Jr., Larry, Ronny, Linda, Carol, Rodney
Moosie, Herbie, Jean, Darrell, Frankie, the little ones, Marie,
Sandy, the other jr, the one in the war, all the lives of our future
all the hearts of our newer bodies, our strength, all the strength

what are there where are there paths are they lives to be lived or
played with or snuffed white man they way go out fast smooth not even
drunk with the world on fire and them on fire in fire on top of fire
FIRE at everybody, and everything that will not move with you
little ones, and kellie and wanda and lisa and vera the little
ones and pavel and accra, and the children of dumber deader faster
men, where will they survive, Charles Jr. and Malika, where
will they live when our houses fall down, what will they say to
each other about us, why will they be sad or happy, who will kiss who
and what will their real faces look like, stripped of the wt of their
mothers and fathers dead now, in the grave, turned, to dirt, and
finer forms.

THE BOOGALOO SONNET(S)

in the stree was betty r, with 5 kidz
in the street was bett, ray, cripple man
miss johnson and kidz missarlene, mis stokes
miz slade, missus wilson, they all missus, but
missus wilso she divorced, living with a hairy
cat.
in the feeling of the stree'song
i heard beautiful ladies with wigs singin
wigs with man holes and saucers cripple man raise his hand
mouths yeh, all the babees we hear, cripple man sees all, and
old mister turnhat. is there death in the red juice
               will the cores cause it
               lying silent as the dog army
               steps through patroling the street
               at night against fattyarbuckle the pimple
               carred face-rider, a dead poison feather
               (he lisp)
               sprawled under each new sun
               with the same dignity
               as their untouched
               turnds
               enormous artifacts

like stones breathing before duhnoo cars comes

FUNKY BUTT, AN AMERICAN NEGRO MISSED-EQUAL PUET

Funky butt, funky butt in the nation
in the army in the saloon enterprise arranging
deranging teaching schul in the amos building
for sanchez motors a crooked leg straightening
enterpise known as "be sumpin pinball before
ocean clean your shit up," before the heavens
lean on your crooked leg crooked eye like an ape
with memorized putdowns, like a hairy vampire
on leave from united artis' funky butt dirty
head, all the same a shame these cats cripblow
want to be captain shitsandwich lowboxing a dog
its all in the way you pronounce your hideousness
it is a picture of corniness funky butt an image
of bebop bill the wagon dragger, dragging his
nosepaper clippings around, showin 'em to loose
jews, and in the airplane factory of he haid
they still got propellers, like an oopiedop machine
which cant stop making oopiedops though oopiedops
have been obsolete since 1945.
Funky butt in the street
funky butt slide
funky tight neck
dirty shirt rolled sucking the juice
from a rolled up dirty
juice tight. Funky
know he cool, he holy
as running sore nectar
elliptical as old feces
funky is free from any
philosophy save funkieism
which be a peepee ladder to
vestville, and dirtyneck city
it also out of style
and like 1945 melodramatic
bebop, gets old, quicker
than slanthumping, which
indeed is tiring, and up
the street kind of noise.

Funky
plus sharkface
and Mandrake the
acidhand killer, hole up
in paradise alley, with
white girls, orange soda,
and tunafish kotex

They have this to say. ME. ME. ME. ME. ME.
which sound like french hole talk.
Or crampus the vampus, the mayor of no where.
They writes and feels, and talks, about black people

(tough shufflers of the new order
canreaders, quoters, stealers, loiterers in dumb smell
They will pass with the rest
of the gas. Hizzoner. Hizzoner. Herr Fuhrer. Herr invisibles
They are the gray vee the turmoil of loss, we need some
roads, some zoom some way to get to the place we feel
not these cripple giblets of unintelligent desire
these stephinfechitiy losers, ask them, they love crap special

INFLUENCE OF

    Black Mind is mine a mine
      for the gold of past and future
        Shine your gold black light
          out of yr mind into the mine
            of our time.
              Be James Brown and wish
                  the line to the mind is straight
                      w/rhythm flyin, change up stride
                    in blinding light

                    And JB be
                      digging
                        out flows black
                        streams black
                        gush black
                          shouting gold
                          force in heaven
                          back above
                          hover
                            strutting
                            ground
                            Bees
                            JB
                            James
                            Brown
                            A rich man
                            A priest of gold

                                          energy figures

black juice royal time
    Brown
    James
    Brown
        floods
        floods
        & gushes
        of energy
        Rivers of movement
        Oceans of Yea-uh

             Oceans of Yea-uh
             Brown
             James
             Oceans
             of
             Yea-uh
In gold green orange and James
In maroon chartreuse silver and Brown
James
J.B.
digging in the black
gold mind

All the world and heavens moan forever
in sweet black angelic Bogaloosence
        yea-uh
        yea-uh
YEA-UH

THE DANCE OF THE TOMS

Here is the dance tom tanz
all the little toms, all in a row
here is roy wilkins with his head in a bag
here is bayard rusty switchin like a fag
all the toms here they go, all the toms, in a row
hello toms hello
where you on your way
hello toms hellow
we know how you get your pay
tom is a sick thing
tom is a dirt sucker
a resistance to goodness
tom flies in metal
tom mama is tom mama
and draws is backwards on a pole
tom know god and hate him
saying hellow to white god for bux
      a vomit eater
  a pansy
    a duck of sausage flake, a failure in the universe with god grading
tom walk backwards all the time to provide evil a opening a hostlike affair
if you go to movies tom will drop down to eat the peanut shells so graytitty
wont have to sweep she stuff he so cool tom he look like television shadow
and some people not sure he actual exist, but he doos

with cape and gun
and strawberry hair
   toom toom where you goin
we gon kill you very soon
we gon break you funkin neck
use your ass to start a warm fire for us
now its cold your master shitty breath make icecicle on the world
      we use your ass to heat stuff
        maybe then we not have to stay in
           counting our childrens grave it bees so
               freezen

TIME FACTOR A PERFECT NON-GAP

all presence requires feeling
can you feel a new reality living
can you be a new reality living
you must be a new reality alive now
you must stop old rot bopping
you can not live as old rot bopping
a new reality alive now
you need a new reality alive now
                      you need a
                      new new new new
                      and on to post now
                          post new

knowing is
reality

Now know past know
knowing is
Reality
And what you blew
is new
is new
is new

NO MATTER, NO MATTER, THE WORLD IS THE WORLD

A broke dead genius
moved on to dust
will touch you one night, the world's
gone stale on you, and women staggering in the great deep sleep
of the negro, the great deadness, the great echoing beer tickles
of breath will inform you of all our future, one night, they will be beating
the walls to find a way to sit on a stoop and die, like beggars for nothing
but what they are, and the stacked dust of a gone brother will hunch you
some father you needed who left you and all his messages tried to be wiped
out by devils, in this now of a nightmare for us, my son is here now, we
can all breathe easier, but one night they will be stacked one million
high up and down the line of lives, dying, and cursing, and backing into
each other's sharpened deadness, killing and lying, and getting strange
headaches in the morning when someone mentions strength or clearheadedness.
In the middle of the confused night
In the middle of the dream of flying tombs and batpeople sucking blood.
The dream will sweat, growing.
A big nigger will kill another big nigger.
Dope will go in somebody elses arm, so help me, a blind man will lead
some more of us down narrow wooden stairs, stumbling into the street,
crawling to his blue airconditioned cadillac. We will all be stumbling and
crawling. And be insane for those few hundred years.
A brother, a father will speak to you.
The voice and will of Allah, God, he will speak to you.
You will be crawling down a tar highway naked and burned, and sucking on
a steering wheel. The car will have crashed. The blind man burning in the
middle of the highway, tracks of zionists, cowboys, mobsters, through his
mashed in creamy skull. Melted wax thoughts make the highway glitter.
Stars of the highway glitter the dead man. He is not Allah. He will hunch
up and die, growing fat, and hysterical, talking to devils in cellars.
It will be your live brother asleep, leading a blind mindless angel into
a cadillac in the act of blowing up, the pieces are stars. Your father will
whisper to you, from far into Allah's breast the way, like a dead broke
genius you will not listen, like a live spasm of Allah you will awake to
the whispering which will be the stars and leaves of heaven's breathing
sensual in your face, you will rise and look around. And the world will
be oozing with righteous devils and the sentries of your mothers selling
ass across the planet, and they will sink down on your mother breathing
heavy in the hallway down the narrow cadillac stairs of the leadership.
You will not know who you are until then in the dust and embarrassment of

his not understanding your big sad eyes, and soft voice. You will be then
the spirit the dead genius speaks to you of, the wind chiming against the
eyes of Allah will echo the wisdom of your rising, and brown body glistening
muscles breaking out everywhere, disrupting air sea transport and lies on
the windowsill of our falling down castles. A spirit will speak to you,
spirit will speak to you, rise, black man, it will say, a spirit will speak
to you, rise black man, it will say, a spirit will, a spirit, will speak,
will speak, will will will speak to you spirit will rise to you say rise
rise rise rise black man, and your beautiful body will shine in actual heaven
your beautiful soul will shine in actual heaven, you will be alive and
awake and moving like you ought to be. You will be everything we have always
wanted, and could not remember to be. Allah will be in you again, Obalaji,
my son, my strong warrior, you will do this for all of us

PRAYER FOR SAVING

Survive and Defend.

Defend and Survive.

Defend the space you live upon Defend your family your way of
   feeling
   about the world. Defend The Impressions
   and Muhammad Ali
   Defend Ray Robinson and the Songhay Empires
   Defend the Pyramids and Huey Newton in the same breath the same
people faced with the same disasters in the physical world, the
emergence of the naked apes on horseback from out the icebox zones

 the squares with paper ears and wooden steps against whom we must defend
in spite of whom we must survive
defend and survive
   let black green and red survive, and the angle of success, pyramid
     let moses appear and be chastised in our songs
   for sleeping around and talking too much
     like Broad Street's liberal niggers
       let our words and music survive
         let The Temptations please let their feeling survive
          Please Black People Defend John Coltrane and Sun Ra
            Claude McKay must survive his long black knowledge walks
          in footprint sands of europe america and westindies must stand
         his banana boats and homes in harlem must be protected at all costs
      and Duke Ellington we must hear him in the 22nd century as
sweetly and the flying images of sound enlightenment his
diminuendos and crescendos must be preserved behind the alleyways and broken
    stoops of Howard Street and Centre Street all the Wattses and
       Houghs must be protected with Duke there and The Vandellas
   recoloring everything in our reach. We must paint these falling
buildings with brilliant moorish arabesques of Ankhs and
   riming love words of Egyptian light and reunderstand that death
is not horrible but merely graduation if we are together into a new
   adventure, in our new more spiritual forms

      Defend the way you walk my man sister tell him to do it
     the coolness like we really meant by cool slow fire protect
   let it survive as the universal oasis of civilization. Build new
     blackbeautiful things. New Shapes

150 /

Buildings . . .
                   l
                    i
               k h i
                e t s   "WILD" STUFF
                           ECSTASY HAPPENINGS
                              sun comes up on a street like kisses

          survive to do your real thing
          defend the energy the hipness in you
          it is too valuable that people everywhere understand
               why we got so many dances
               why we like colors
          why we able to run so fast and fight so hard
       why jimmy brown cd carry six dudes on his back for forty yards
       and beat five outta his way
            this must rise all of it, jimmie's runs must televise movie
       reality in fast and slowmotion for ever till change makes it new
     jimmy name amunubi rakaptah or some future black rich swiftness
          like it, city
                    must mean 40 yards beatin dudes off him
                    music must have ground crushed sun walls
                    screams in the woodwork in orange and blue

                    mayor must mean big black holy man
                         must mean again, a prince
                              blessed with the wisdom of a strong people

                    Survive
                    and Defend
                    Survive
                    and Defend

       suedes and maroon pants
     warm breeze over some kinda other brown
     in the bed listening to each other breathe
               those smiles of
               our women and giggles of
               our running children
               their brilliant drinkknowledge eyes

/   151

    Survive
and Defend. Draw around fight to the end
        The end of SquareWorship
        and Ugliness. The end of
        Corniness, and meat selfishness

    Survive
and Defend all these things in us
All These Things We Are
Or Come From

            Survive Survive Survive and Defend

            Survive Survive Survive and Defend

            Spirit of Black Life

            Live in Eternity

FOLKS.

Dont
bite
the
nite
a white
"man"
mite
own
it.

                        (so what?
                       so what?
                   so oooo ooo ooo oooo
                                     ooooo
                                          oooooo
                                              ooooo
                                                  o
                                                  o
                                           o
                                    o
               o
               o
                 oooo
                      ooo
                o o
                   o oo
                     oo
                 o
            oooo
            o ooo
       oo   o
       o
   oo
ooo
  oo
    oooooo
     oo
      oooo
       oooo

                              oo
                                ooo
                                  oo
                                    oo
                                      oo
                                          what?
bite
the
muthafucka
a n y waaaaaaaaaaaaaaaaaaaa aaaaaay

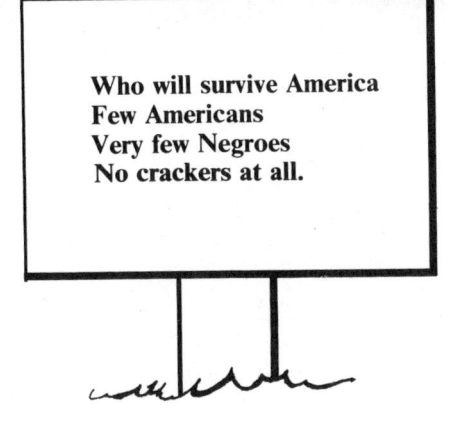

> **Who will survive America**
> **Few Americans**
> **Very few Negroes**
> **No crackers at all.**

Who will survive America?
Few Americans
Very few Negroes
No crackers at all.

Will you survive America,
with your 20cent habbit,
your fo' bag jones, will you
survive in the heat and fire
of actual change? I doubt it

Will you survive woman? Or will yo nylon wig
catchafire at midnight, and light up Stirling Street
and your assprints on the pavement. Grease meltin in this
brother's eyes, his profile shotup by a Simba thinking
who was coming around the corner was *really* Tony Curtis, and not a
misguided brother, got his mind hanging out with Italians.

Who will survive
the black future
will. You cant with the fat stomach between your ears
scraping nickels out the inside of nigger daydreams.
Few Americans
Very few Negroes ... maybe no Red Negroes
at all.
      The stiffbacked chalklady baptist, in blue lace
      if she shrinks from blackness in front of the church

/ 155

    following the wedding of the yellow robots
    will not survive. She is old anyway, and they're moving
    her church in the wind.
    Old people. No.
    Christians. No.
    First Negroes To Be Invisible To Truth. 1944. Minnesota. No.
Nothing of that
will be any where.
It will be burned clean.
It might sink and steam up the sea. America might. And no Americans
very few Negroes, will get out. No crackers at
all.

But the black man will survive America.
His survival will mean the death of America.
Survive Blackman! Survive Blackman! Survive Blackman!
(Black woman
too.)
    Let us all survive, who need
    to. OK. And we wish each other
    luck!

REALITY IS DEALT WITH

Dealt with reality is better to be with
Without dealing with reality nothing is sure
Be sure to be in reality
Be sure your plans are reality.
Is Joe Tex in a real world?
Ask Joe Tex. Is Texas in a real world. Well, only
partially.
Reality
What is around
What abounds from all out the ground
What you bees around, the real the answers the cold wall the
warm heart, deal with it. Deal with the splash of claws calls itself
a wind or woman deal with that.

What you want to happen can only happen in reality
What you want to be you can only really be in reality
Dream world sideways
Dream world full of shadows and edges
Faces and hands in the real world
Words words in the real world are real words names of things
      names of
        Actions, doings, ongoing realities
   Nothing is worth nothing save in reality
  I want the world a beautiful reality
And everyone alive in it in love with beautiful reality
   And reality God truth, what ever you dig to say about it,
     tho you dig that saying deals not save in reality
      through realities . . . dont get away from that . . . reality
     that we all must work to force reality into reality

"Dazed and out of their wool heads . . ."

The conquered, the prisoners, stand in line
to watch what they're ordered to watch, it could be
the moon, the evilest of selves, the pretender to light like
the master of artificial science himself, the synthesizer, himself
synthesized, a synthesis, a sin thesis, of all the negative elements
all the opposites possible in creation. You have moon-man, the cracker
Whom the dazed and conquered submit to every day. Beneath their own gaze
beneath the gaze of their own God, they still submit to moonman. They
act like moonman, look like they think moonman look, talk like moonman,
lo and behold they will stand up in front of moonman and tell moonman they
hate him, when it is moonman with his jaded lacklight self completing the
sentence with heavy stick infested breathing, being his own kicks and kick-
er moonman moonmaid moonteeth pronged through living breathing young
animals dazed animals drugged animals duped animals animals with contracts
animals with degrees animals licking on other animals involved with the graceless killer
　reflection
of their own potential eminence because they will not emanate from themselves
but use the killer darts the sticks the iron bars sunk in moonman's eyes
as their lightning, when the heavens are full of legitimate lightning
when the prisoners heads are full of electrical vibrations jumping right
out of they wool thick skies. The moon has them hypnotized. Watching the
killer beings emerge cloaked in bloodthoughts and maniacal whines, beneath
themselves, as emanations from themselves, the beastly moon eat up their
eyes mess up their skies, twists the prisoners' blackfeeling minds

the moon

lies

in the heavens

it is only a beatle

imitating

Otis Redding (an insect trying to be a man)

Oh my dazed and imprisoned brothers

Sunpeople out of whose insides all warmth and light are created

Be your selves Be your self all selves into that big burning

Holy One

Make it bright day for us all, so we can see better and be warm and happy

Be your self again, Son, Light up this dark old world

WHAS GON HAPPEN

Land
will change
hand
s

Where pigs rule now/soon
the
"coon"
in a changed up groove
will
be
the man/be
his ol
black
self

Land
will change
hand
sss

Lives
will be took
will be lost
& gained
but Bloods
will see
again
will know
again

Will be even hipper
than they are now
if you can stan'
it

Land
will change
hand
s

All the pieces
drawn together
puzzle
nigger
solved
by his self

A   merica
will break up
into a hundred pieces
& Bloods will stand black whole bad swift cool fine

in they
own
land (mind)
s
& draw them
Pan-Afro Garvey Dubois Nkrumah style
into One

IN THE YEAR

In the year of reconstruction, 1969, we turn again
to look at our selves, turn again to old understanding
experience colors the landscape reality color, curtains of words
trap dreams like objects
a suicide name America
breathes farts on our momentary conclusions
so turn again
rear up again
the thing we need, is each other
if we could find completion as sand lays cool for the rising
wave
a natural
dependence
on what already exists

though the tide returns each night
and the earth speeds through space
they hook up just the same

FOR MAULANA KARENGA & PHAROAH SANDERS

The body of man is evolved to a brain
and speech, in the dark, a drum, thru
forests and over water, speech, man
with his black self, describes the
sea and forest, the trails of earth
and sinewy flying things, the pyramid
of his life, begins to describe
what is in him, beating image off his tongue,
the blood, carrying image thru the heart, the blood
himself, on a lake, with his, wo-man, the blood, then,
in his black eloquence, described, that, wo-man

speech, the drum creates
life as the heart, sees, and makes
itself, a life, and again, a life, like the holy sun
with us for ever, then another, past that.

Describe beauty brother-lover, create worlds of dazzling sweet color
Speech, image in the sand, the water pulls up, cloud sketch a colony
of other kinds of life, rain waving thru the middle air, as a heart
describes,

the momentary taste of picture
the God Thot
arrived
sweet seeing
and then, behind that,
we did another thing

we began
to sing

(PRIEST POEM)

A Lecture Past Dead Cats

(Scatter energy little holes too small to be what shd be)

        What shd be is
        what we gonna do
        how we gonna move
        in the right direction
O nation of super hip swift motional creation
O people of natural sweet smoothness
O Beings of the double clutch   G
            the attitude   E
            the slide   S
            the fake   T
            the stuff   U
            the slow hang in the air   R
O delicate vibratories of ecstatic madness shimmering   E
in falsetto worship spires of cool goodness
O tone carriers of glowing magic
            of sudden stops
            & jiggles
O spangle of cosmic prepostelectronic color
Black mohair spirits
Evolutional saviours of the worth of humanity
   (if it is to be considered as worthy
     of divinity
O nearest interpreters of divinity and regality
O beautiful sounds of the existent

It is an honor to be one of your priests
Let us commune in our hooked up downness, our consummate bad ness
as together specimens
of laughing magic
Let us gesture the invisible symbols of constant creation
HEY HEY HEY!!!

It is an honor to be one of the priests
One of the blessed.

Teach

NOTHING MORE TO SAY

There is nothing more to say
do, do that and do do do that
no more say
no more, do it, gwan do it do it
it needs to be done, needs to be
done, do your needs, to be done
desires fall behind, needs nothing
but past saying its do it do it

OCTOBER 1969

    I look up from my 12 year old's nod
    and I am 35, an old young man.
Already mid life yet full of the same longing
The never to be completed ripening Oh I yearn
for completion and new life the will of it
rips out of me
reach out of me for you gentle girl

I have seen many suns
rise
the endless succession of hours
piled upon each other
the words pass
between ancient baby mouths
cards of life image flip fast change
and still I'm full of wonder
to love to see
to want to have more than description or
feeling
This half life stalled upon a time
the very hour of cross road and new commitment
25 years from now
I will be 60
an old grey black sage
I swear now upon the seven secret elements
(the bones of lords known and
unknown)
to keep my purity of purpose
to cultivate courage and will
   to righteous grow(n) into a nation's
spiritual carpenter
my apron's blueprints
((the poet-warrior-statesman
grown together
a burning jewel of flame
at the very top of the pyramid
If we are together then
as we must certain be
come pat my bushy head
nice old man

nice old man
you will be fortunate
by such act
as will give you a permanent understanding
of my long eventful
moment
praising god on this
planet

ASK ME WHAT I AM

The rhythm of beings is the reason for
being. The sanity of form is allness wholeness rightness
nigger love a magic being
the dipping interior resurrect constant continuous
the way the nigger walk

the red hat is a magic hat
the razor a sword flasher
the lines of adepts all niggers really
the pyramid speaks of niggers actually
the word will be given to niggers
we are in our most holy selves niggers
the nigger is a midget god constructed of rhythm and gism
we are in our most holy selves niggers
god is a nigger really
ask who god is and he will answer if you ask right

nigger is a definition of the wholly detached from material consideration
a nigger dont have no gold
not even a negro got gold but a negro think like he wd if he had gold
a nigger is holy
a nigger is killer and builder struts frantic for love
nigger is a frantic love man hippity hoppity 7 sided figure
the nigger who i am
who is my self and father mother your self
deep man
my man

my main man
my main main man

we niggers together
forever

raise.

NIXON

with his pointed head
a dignified deadbeat, with EUREKA
a job,
better than the one in the grocery store
or the one as Insurance Spider
or the one biting teeny girls' putties
Dusty Brown Suit
Congealed Hair Saluting
Dont sit near guys like that anywhere
They'll disturb you if you intelligent
Bore you if you life-ridden
EUREKA
this one got a job a dull wrinkled salesman
with nothing
to sell. Hey Dick
HEY DICK NIXON
you a dull ass
muthafucka

THE METROPOLIS OF DEPRAVED BEINGS

They will always
get a nigger
to have his finger
on the trigger—

TANGUHPAY

The world speaks, and we, the blood, the main men of nature
feel the buzz, the light high of consciousness pouring in
we slide across what isss, speak world, hey, the light high
the pursuit of, yes, light, itself, the sun of a holy being.
The world speaks
and we find our selves
where are we, where were we, find our
selves, strung out in jesus land, spose to stake out a claim,
and we blind, on low adventure, for centuries now we dont even know
the name
of the game
the world speaks, my ears
         buzz
         your ears, beautiful dreamers
         let em open up too

get a buzz on off knowledge
a knowledge buzz
find out what is and what was
history a slow walkin shiny suit wearin dude
will tell you a story you might cant do without
—
The world speaks
are we in, can we listen to these tunes
can we, know know why they mouth is pointed at a star whose us
can we, shinin, can we, turnin slow and slow, can we feel from know
whose words, if words words can have a truly owner, a owner
other than every thing. When the yes, the world, speaks
and your ears opend up listening describe a brightness like the magic drum
of invisible wings, yes, fly fly, the world is rapping, get down with it, listen

Thas the truth
oh, the truth
our worshipd name, yeh, for speakin a listener grows
oh, said true true true, the truth
was speakin
like a nice song
you know
like a very very nice song

WE ARE HERE

We are here
caught up in some such
situ   a   shun
And we gon get what we can
get, and do what we can
do
we are *actually* here
actually for real can you hear me
up tight
and not in the abstract philosophical marshmallow
of some dying sensibility

we are actually here, where you can see and feel us
if you could see
or feel
and we must have something
we must reach something
here where we are now, on this street with the sun
midpoint in the sky, and my brother screaming in the front room
we must have something
something real
and that is what we want

INTEREST CIRCULATING

No face stares from the dark
you recognize yrself
you recognize the dark
all together flows silent magic
will it speak? Ask the face
its name. Will it answer?
Ask the face
to sing or something. It will not
It is a looker probably
It just looks probably
Well ask it what it sees
It wont answer. Why. It wont
answer. Why? Why? Thats your
question. No one else,
is speaking.

WHY DIDNT HE TELL ME THE WHOLE TRUTH

I'll give you a silver dollar
if you'll learn The Creation.
Why eyes. Big eyes. My mother
had me saying The Gettysburg Address
in a boyscout suit. Why didnt you say
something else, old man. I never learned
by heart, The Creation, and that is the key
to all life. I strain now through the mists
of other life, to recall that old man's presence.
I know we are linked in destiny and cause.
I know he my guardian and deepest teacher.
I stand on his invisible shoulders.
I look for his enemies to tear their throats.
I wish that he had told me about J. A. Rogers and
Psychopathia Sexualis. I wish he had showed me
his Mason Book.
Perhaps it would have meant another path.
It wda saved some time, some energy, some pain.
But love is the answer we keep saying, only love.
And in my grandfathers pained eyes I remember only
the keen glint of divine magnetism. My grandfather
loved me.

AFRICA AFRICA AFRICA

Africa Africa Africa
Africans Africa Africans Africa
African African Africa Africa
Africans Africa Africans Africa
Africa
Africa
Ahoo
Ahooooo hoooo
Ahoo
Ahooooo hoooo
Africa
Africa
Africa
beat it in your mouth
beat it through your veins
beat it in the green earth, your mother
beat it in the tall forests, that grab for the sun
in the pavement places
Africa
((Africa))
in the turn of narrow tenements where boogaloo grows ((Africa
in the insane scream and slide outtasight ((the sun halfhid
by the world it nourishes,
      Africa
      Africa
      We are a whole people
      We are a whole gorgeous people
      We are Africans
      A Whole People A Holy People
      We are Africans
      A Whole People
      Never forget this dancer
      A whole people, where ever in this
      solar system, we are the soul of the
      whole
      system
      Africans
      Our land, wherever we are,
      Africa

Tho we claim whatever space our
righteous selves have died upon
we are no colorless landlords ((the land is the workers
                              the nation's legacy
                              We want all of the Africans
                              to reach out for each other
We want all of the Africans to lock arms with each other
We want all of the Africans to move closer, look in the same direction,
and move in the same move to claim what they need to survive in cold space
                              We are the Africans
                              You understand? The Africans
        Ah, you remember us? The Africans. Yes. The Children
of The Sun. Africans
Yes. Africans.
Yes. Africans,
    Africans,
    Africans

THE WORLD IS MY POEM

Poetry is not the sole means of my expression
my life is such a broad thing
stretched out in all directions.
The poem now is a note of flying energies. Speeding meat hums
of the evolving organism. The music becomes straighter, a clearer
melody, the harmonies worked out to a single multicolored tone.
A postcoltrane anthemic national image. The words of the old folks
the sound of our new selves, a theme revolving in meaning forever
even if our sun explodes. We deal with the reason past the reasons.
We mean what is after all the seen and felt by the totality of what
   has ever been.
On a street in a Newark slum. Central Ward, November 1969, in the reign
of Pig Richard the faggot hearted, I speak out of a need to communicate
with the yet unborn nations of righteousness. From the most ancient
people on this planet. Now slaves, many unconscious, as a warrior-poet
of the age. This writing is a warning of how far creation can be stretched
to include absolute evil, and absolute delusion. Power must have a balance
It must include the positive evolution of all the forces.

BUNNIES

Bangs and kills in an old street
drummers talking, slick exits,
jungle stacked up parade, shy
hair and lights, co-neoned
at sundown
           You will be everywhere
           the talked to, the pointed at
           they all remember your vanished
           photograph.

We used to think
Death was an old play
on television. And those character actors
before sound
were magnificent

2.

   These cd be hills floating like
ghosts
in the emptiness
of the world

in this flicker
settle, hang un
happy in cold wind

The streets are seas
with changing
lights

3.

Speeds
as wide as their
paths.

Outlines of trees
and an honest green
in the flashes

In the heartlessness of stiff dawn
they cd lay in the warmth of each other's breath.

They cd possess themselves, and the man, finally
get the woman to do what he had asked her

She instead, wd be, and he, and the world,
and the pitiful sunshine in children's books

wd sputter
and go out

PROFOUND IS LOST LIKE EVERYTHING ELSE

There are more lies
in print
more fools
on lose
on coins
as heads of
indians
as dying jingles
wit th fat sttoomaks
wit the jowls of the end 'a me
with the singing squelled, up in there
way up in there
knotty haid fools
bent on sun shine mirror
of tin sef
walks hunched over
preys to he sef
fly
if he cd
caint
this motherfucker
will hang out wit you
talk his shit
steal from you
then walk around talking about babies
this is the atom of the future
dont hate evil
swim in it call it what you can to make you bigtop
he wd
we wd
they wd
decline the detention the declension
of the mulattoes

My people are beautiful anyway and they can fly
We may not be the self conscious few who want to be god
while god hesef is among us walks who we wd lift, and he is the lifter
in trouble, in danger, in the heat of decline and failure this is god
what can be don what can we see god is dead no he is in chains and
sweeps out white folks yards. o say o say os say osay the god

i need, god the god you need we want to be and god
is the whole but a bent black man without anything
even an opinion

CAREERS

What is the life
of the old lady
standing
on the stair
print flowered
housedress
gray and orange
hair
bent
on a rail
eyes open for
jr.
bobby
jb, somebody
to come, and carry her
wish
slow
cripple woman, still does
white folks work
in the mornings she get up
creeps into a cadillac
up into the florient lilac titty valleys
of blind ugliness, you think the woman loves
the younger white woman
the woman she ladles soup for
the radio she turns on when the white lady nods
she carries them in her bowed back hunched face
my grandmother workd the same
but stole things for jesus' sake
we wore boss rags in grammar school
straight off the backs of straight up americans
used but groovy and my grandmother when she returned at night
with mason jars and hat boxes full of goods
probably asked for forgiveness on the bus
i think the lady across from me must do the same
though she comes back in a cab, so times, it seems,
have changed.

THE MINUTE OF CONSCIOUSNESS

You pay for it, for sure, dont let nobody tell you you don. You pay.
In all the ways, possible, through the traps, moon light traps, collecting
absences, and kisses, lovers trail through the imagination lighting fires
throughout the civilized world, destroying primitive man's "progress"
to the obeisances of spirit, the salary of the blind.

It is a path song. Mountains pass under and over, cold birds turn to blink.
A rope hung from way up, tied to a leader, a spirit, a system, an old teacher
himself, tied up higher movn just a lil higher.

Sometimes you want to know is it worth it. The deprivation, the trying
narrow decision, move on, move on. You want to know sometimes when the world
beat down around you, the planet groans from so much pain, the pointless
murders and idiot laughter from the merv griffin show, then you know that

what you do is what the ancestors prepared you for. The lighting of the flame
The moving of the rock. The shouting out of the great names, the great
national spirits. Then the feeling in tuned and turned slowly our turn itself

hits a certain note, mighty pythagoras, the sound, the color.

WHAT ARE YOU WAITING FOR?

The judgement of morning, is to be cool
and light blue
itself, wishing for more sun
leaning toward the total screaming eruption
of noon
the army of dogs
patroling outside the colored folks houses
the sabbath it is quieter, just before the clean clothes
get put on
and the devil who is less visible today
as we take the streets in waves of color
going to worship a stranger's god
would that the ancient gods would come out
you could jump up for freedom then yo god wdnt let you be no slave
pink lady
red lady
green and yellow lady, way down the steet
leather coats comin off the printing press now
high and low dresses, sickness
all coming off the printing press now
along with civil rights
and assimilation, and whiter than white, is righter than
right
right
on
And return from under the oldest underseer's moneyloving rubberlips
we nigger baptists and methodists and catholics and radicals and other figures of
halting speech the newest leech to rob us blind and sic us on ourselves
is alive and well in animal paradise
It is easter, or christmas, no it is the day of commemoration of Malcolm
X's assassination.

THE STORY OF THE BLACK MAN IS A FUNNY STORY

If you can laugh, for centuries
then stop, till the devil dies, then

laugh some more at the sudden light,
the powertowers of suns piled onto suns

and the eye of the mighty lord beaming at our growth
towards the giant self of the cosmos—pray

the end of our suffering is near, make us move it thru worthiness
the end of hatred and ugliness, can you hear me, the end of stupidity

is soon, we have willed it, teach, feel the germinative atoms stretch out
and change vi-bration,

the coming liberation of the ancient sun-worshipers

the reunderstanding by the colored people that they are the new life of the planet

    We will make earth a model, what is its real name, ((What is your real name

    A natural artifact of the creative intelligence
    when you approach the planet you will hear us singing

    you will hear the planet itself whispering its love for the solar system

    we will have caught the sun in the roofs of our temples

    and the engines like mingling hearts produce the philosophy

    the flower like love engines produce the philosophy

    the people, hear, peop-le, at one with the universal energy

    they are praying now, the middle of the day, hover for a second

    in rhythmic meditation

    now descend to greet us stranger

a red dude from mars, a blue trumpet player from Saturn

at the next stage, words coalesce as slow tingling gas

at the next light, a nucleus of exchanging wisdoms, A chanting furnace

all go round, all go round, all go round, its laughter you hear

a big laughter, all beyond the zillionth planet

and now we have become part of that laughter

the shaking roar

our insides glitter, like the atomic furnace of our sky heater

your heart sees

we are   together

REALITY

from somewhere a
per-some
holy where
this per per
reality breaks down
you know-ooooo
breaks in like a murderer
breaks thru crazy words
from somewhere we were walking
i had told you another time what we needed
from somewhere
the sun watched us .

Ooooo
the things we need
beat on head, our brothers lie
their ego in this white nation saved to kill their selves ooo
from somewhere we needed
needed each other, loving
we wanted wanted this to be reality
we wanted it for everybody, and maybe this was wrong
to want truth from liars
and grace from the wholly
fallen

IT'S
NATION
TIME

THE NATION IS LIKE OURSELVES

The nation is like our selves, together
seen in our various scenes, sets where ever we are
what ever we are doing, is what the nation
is
doing
or
not doing
is what the nation
is
being
or
not being

Our nation sits on stoops and watches airplanes take off
our nation is kneeling in the snow bleeding through 6 layers
of jewish enterprise
our nation is standing in line ashamed in its marrow for being
our nation
a people without knowledge of itself
dead matter we are thrown on the soil to richen
european fields
the dead negro is fertilizer
for the glorious western harvest
our nation is ourselves, under the steel talons
of the glorious
Devil
our secret lover who tells us what to do
the steel orange eyes
the ripping fingers of
the Devil
who tells us what to do
blondie
your dress so high
wallachs nigger
mod nigger
nigger in a cow boy hat
why you want to be a cow boy
laid up with a cow

he shouts "power to the nipples,"
doctor nigger, please do some somethin on we

lawyer nigger, please pass some laws about us
liberated nigger with the stringy haired mind, please lib lib lib
you spliv er ate
US, we you, coo-
lust dancing thru yr wet look
ing
tent
acles
please mister liberated nigger love chil nigger
nigger in a bellbottom bell some psychedelic wayoutness
on YO People, even while freeing THE People, please
just first free YO people, ol marijuana jesus I dug your last
    record
with the hootenany biscuits, was revolutionary as a
    motherfucker, ple
ple please mister kinkyman, use your suntan susan swartz is
    using
it, her and tom jones on their show with you and diane carroll
    tiny ti
mmm and the newest negro to understand that theres no black
    no white
only people . . .
    yo imagination is fabulous, reverend, pray for color
    peeples, when the mayor or after the mayor or before
    duh mayor give you yo check, please reverend, and
        daddyboy
and tonto greengrits, and pablo douchebag, susan goldberg's
    daring
nongringo, and allthekidstogether . . . reach back to the constant
    silence
in our lives, where the ideas line up to be graded, and get a
    better one
going than we got, for you and me,
please mr new thing
please mr mystical smasheroo just under ¼ strength learning
    about it
from the flying dutchman
please mr ethnic meditations professor profess your love for black
people we waiting

while you say right on and commit the actual take over of
    yourself

in the anteroom of anything, just before or just after anything
trudging down the halls of your wifes straightened haid we
 realize
how tough things are and how you cant alienate the people
 with the
money we live among stars and angels, listen to devils whines
 like
cold space between the planets, we know
the turn in the hall, your visit to the phone booth to put on an
inferior man suit
a super animal trump
the tarts of your individual consciousness
please all you individuals
and would be involved if people were nicer to you types
or frightened of the military aspects of national liberation folks
in your reinvolved consciousness flitting over the sea at jamaica
if the rastafarians dont kill you please mr vacationing writer
 man
write some heavy justice
about black people
we waiting
we starved for your realness
we know you on the move now
we heard you was outside cairo
bathing at a spa
please mr world travler
please mr celebrity, mr nigger in the treasury department
mr disc jockey for the mournful cash register of the nigger soul
please mr all of us
please miss lady bug
oh lady oh brother, wherever and who ever you are
breathing on
oh please please in the night time
more please in the mewning
we need need you bbbaby man, we need all the blood we gotta
get some blood and
you in your wilderness blood
is the nigger
yes the sweet lost nigger
    you are our nation sick ass assimilado
        please come back
            like james brown say
                please please please

SERMON FOR OUR MATURITY

We want to be all we can
we want to know all we can
we want to feel all we can
all there is
all there was
all there will evoooooo
            be   ("Here come d' judge"
Can all be the judge   all is the judge)
all *is* the judge

all there is is the judge

We want you to feel it too
We want you to know its you
We in the mountains all in the air
We want to be all over everywhere
Can you feel it too
We want to communicate with you

The motion of love has animated us

We still luv-you-ooooo-oo-oo-oooo-oooo
Theres no way to get out the world
without love—unless you the devil
Theres no connective fabric to the universe
stronger than the atomic magnetism of
   spiritual love
There is only the lover, as a compact
universe, in constant motion
The planets are in constant prayer
The sun is the God they pray to
We are the suns children
Black creatures of grace—
Praise your ancestors thru whom
you came to this planet
attached to a chord from beginning
to now
The seven tones of the scale
are the flying planes of life
Earth men and Earth songs

Play the scale of life, wind
Let us move from plane to plane
We drift in space
as circles of feeling
All the presence of invisible influence
controls the paths we take
Make the invisible visible
   (within yr space
See the things you need to see
and knew they exist
The world shapes and is to be shaped
A portrait of "God" is the universe
alive and conscious down to its
minuteness and finality
Your relationship with all the things
the seen
and the un seen
the felt
and the need to be felt uh

                          ray
                                touch me
              touched pulled thru ether
              speed eater space lover

you need to get better uh
you need to experience better times Negro
We love you negro Love you betta
if you got betta
Love yrself betta
if you got betta

We want to see you again as ruler of your own space
Big Negro
Big ol Negro
        growin
           wind storm flyin thru
           your huge blues lung
   Lung filled with hurricanes
   of transparent fingerpops
   and need to be changed up moans
Stretch out negro
            Grow "Gro
            Gwan "Gro Grow

Stretch out Expand
Bigger than a white boys shack
You the star nee-gro, you touch all points
w / yr circular self

Adam-Atom
is your name
The basic blood
the whole of life
is based upon

Grown up thru these shittyshitties
Aint no Italian suit can contain you
    Yr body is all space
    Yr feet is valley makers
Aint no Italian shoes can contain them
You a black foot Buddha face
Only dancer squat centuries in the desert
    for heavy Simba Training

You can dance Nigger I know it
Dance on to freedom
You can sing Nigger sing
Sing about your pure movement
in space
Grow
You pierced the clouds
of animal ignorance
you bigger than animal cages
yr arms cross the serpent of unknowing
yr heart is Africa and blood line
sweetens the rest of existence
w / color
All color heat and speed
are yours
Salaam Brother
You still
gettin up!!

Bigger than sky scrapers
sunset advertise yr family
in they casual trip to Earth
Yes Ham
You bigger than Negro

Yes Moses, its allright, you raised
meateater off all fours, yr experiment
while dangerous, taught us about
matter and the feelings of the breathing
opposites
We have the experience
We came to the West
We grew in the West
We know the heart of stone
We can talk stone talk
We know about emptiness, hollowness,
blankness, coldness, materialism
and the worship of Gray ness
We have been exposed to Graynesss
We know about witches and Devils
We past that
We grown past animals
We been humans
Not gon' call you Negro if you keep gettin up
Yes, you grown Blood
Your Afro dealin w / images in outter space
Soft million tipped antenna
Bring back and feed on the new images
The new learning Yes
The New Learning is here
Vision thru Afro Antenna
Bloodline got heaven spread out
like evening covering the world
Bloodline from Africa got Yessassss as its sound
slidin thru veins as receivers
Each hair Receive
Each pore Receive
Each space full, praying
fingers praying
arms, lips, hair praying

Not gon' call you Negro if you keep
    gettin up
You grown Blood
fly thru body
feed the planes of feeling
you growin blood
and space in ecstasy to receive you
Heaven got to grow to have you in it you found

out so much truth
you past little eyes and little words
you a shadow to the half blind and a mountain
to the ignorant
Language at celestial altitudes sounds
like bloods scattin at hightempos

Ommmm Mane Padme Hummmmmmm
Ooshoobee doo bee
Ashadu an la Illaha Illala
Ooshoobee doo bee
Tuna Jaribu Kuwa Weusi Tu
Ooshoo bee doo bee
Kiss Venus for me while you up there man
A Huge Black Star
Spread out fireloined in empty space
I hear you laughin man its that hip to be
that hip
You a star and a life sign
You the knower (Noah) that first perceived
the light and made the symbol
We carry yet. Man and his luniverse
at the dawn of creation.

Bring back angelic definition
for our lives here beneath
the mantle of Thing love.

(1) *DIVINE*
     is name We give you
(2) *GRACE*
     is name we give you
(3) *MESSENGER*
     we call you
(4) *PROPHET*
     we call you
(5) *NOBLE BLACK MAN*
(6) *PROFESSOR*
     of Wisdomic Faith
(7) *"MASTER TEACHER,"* father of the new dispensation
     Your growth is our own

   Sifa ote mtu weusi (repeat)

IT'S NATION TIME

Time to get
together
time to be one strong fast black energy space
        one pulsating positive magnetism, rising
time to get up and
be
come
be
come, time to
      be come
      time to
      get up be come
      black genius rise in spirit muscle
      sun man get up rise heart of universes to be
future of the world
the black man is the future of the world
be come
rise up
future of the black genius spirit reality
      move
      from crushed roach back
      from dead snake head
      from wig funeral in slowmotion
      from dancing teeth and coward tip
      from jibberjabber patme boss patme smmich
when the brothers strike niggers come out
come out niggers
when the brothers take over the school
help niggers
come out niggers
all niggers negroes must change up
come together in unity unify
for nation time
it's nation time . . .
                Boom
                Booom
                BOOOM
                Boom
                Dadadadadadadadadadad
                Boom

                              Boom
                              Boom
                              Boom
                              Dadadadad adadadad
                                              Hey aheee   (soft)
                                              Hey ahheee (loud)
                                  Boom
                                  Boom
                                  Boom
sing a get up time to nationfy
singaa miracle fire light
sing a airplane invisibility for the jesus niggers come from the
    grave
for the jesus niggers dead in the cave, rose up, passt jewjuice
on shadow world
raise up christ nigger
Christ was black
krishna was black shango was black
             black jesus nigger come out and strike
                 come out and strike boom boom
                       Heyahheeee come out
                  strike close ford
                       close prudential burn the policies
                    tear glasses off dead statue puppets even those
                          they imitate life
                              Shango budda black
                         hermes rasis black
                            moses krishna
                                       black
when the brothers wanna stop animals
come out niggers come out
come out niggers niggers niggers come out
help us stop the devil
help us build a new world

niggers come out, brothers are we
    with you and your sons your daughters are ours
       and we are the same, all the blackness from one black allah
          when the world is clear you'll be with us
             come out niggers come out

                                                        / 199

        come out niggers come out
It's nation time eye ime
        It's nation ti eye ime
                chant with bells and drum
                it's nation time

It's nation time, get up santa claus   (repeat)
  it's nation time, build it
    get up muffet dragger
      get up rastus for real to be rasta farari
      ras jua
        get up got here bow

                It's Nation
                Time!

SPIRIT
REACH

DERANGED GUTBUCKET PIGTONGUE CLAPPER HEART.

Beats now from
misshaped by the beating on the outside misshaped and beat from
outside misshaped and beat by everything, which is god, ra,
                                                      everything
to keep from naming all the names there are which is god, Obatala,
                                                                                    ra,
allah, to keep from using up all the no time and time and no space
                                                                         and
space to keep from that say, god, allah, everything, all things,
together, that beats
the nigger
that beats him
everything is magnetized to keep him locked to the ground
the pain of final evolution, when we will change, some to gods
some to ashes, some through horror some through ecstasy, boplution,
wayoutistically we will become what we are inside moving to be
cracker you may be wood
and fire is what you need
to change your wooden ways
nigger you might be fire
and need to burn some wood
to live real bright and strong
like you should . . .
                        but
                      maybe
                  may be you wood too—nigger slick butt
               turned around blonde twist on yo ass
            and here you are bein wood
        steada something
     good, Well you get burned too
        or if you fire and wont burn wood you might just
burn yourself, burn more fire, just eat fire eat fire eat fire
till you burn out, cause everything can burn fire out
     everything can beat fire, everything can beat fire's ass
cause allah be beatin be beatin be beatin
cause olorun be beatin yo ass all the time, burnin and burnin
you, allah, be beatin, olorun he be beatin, obatala, be beatin yo
ass
olorun be beatin and allah he be beatin obatala be beatin

and burnin he be all they all be beatin all all all
be beatin
allah, olorun, ra, obatala, they all be beatin
you, nigger, they all be beatin yo ass
till you
change

STUDY PEACE

Out of the shadow, I am come in to you whole a black holy man
whole of heaven in my hand in my head look out two yeas to ice
what does not belong in the universe of humanity and love. I am
the black magician you have heard of, you knew was on you in you
                                                                                           now
my whole self, which is the star beneath the knower's arc, when the
                                                                                        star it
self rose and its light illuminated the first prophet, the five pointed
                                                                                          being
of love.
I have come through my senses
The five the six the fourteen
of them. And I am a fourteen point star
of the cosmic stage, spinning in my appointed orbit
giving orders to my dreams, ordering my imagination
that the world it gives birth to is the beautiful quranic vision

We are phantoms and visions, ourselves
Some star's projection, some sun's growth beneath that holy star
And all the other worlds there are exist alive beneath their own
                                                                              beautiful fires

real and alive, just as we are
beings of the star's mind
images cast against the eternally shifting
heavens.

PEACE IN PLACE

TIME AFTER TIME AFTER TIME AFTER TIME
AFTER TIME
AFTER TIME
AFTER TIME AFTER TIME AFTER TIME A LIE
TIME ALIE
AFTER A LIE TIME
AFTER A TIME, A LIE
AFTER LYING TIMING LIETIME AFTER ALL TIME IS A LIE
LIE AFTER TIME GO AFTER TIME LIE LIE IN TIME LYING
THERE IS WORK TO DO DO YOU SEE IT DO YOU KNOW HOW MUCH WORK
THERE IS TO DO
TO WORK TO WORK THERE IS AFTER TIME WORK AFTER LIES WORK
WILL YOU WORK PAST TIME WILL YOU LIE PAST WORK OR WORK
    OR WORK REAL
WORK REAL WORK BEATS LIE TIME TIME LIES DEAD WORK CAN
WORKING IN TIME
WORKING ALL THE TIME
WORKING THROUGH TIME, PAST IT, DEAL WITH THE GREAT ENSIDERGEE
FIREFINGERS . . . GOLDSPARKS . . . ELECTRIC HAIR . . . EYEBURSTS . . .
    CRACKLE
SPACKLE EYEBURSTS . . . FIREFINGERS
NET GOD SPREAD BURSTS FIREFINGERS THREADHEAT PUNCTURE
HOTPUNCTURES
HOTPUNCTURES
HOTPUNCTURES
HOTPUNCTURES ARE EYEBURSTS AND FIREFINGERS
CRACKLESPACKLE EYEBURSTS ARE FIREFINGERS . . . DEADTIME
                                       . . . NO IMAGE
                              CRAKKKK CRAKK
             CRAKK CRAKK CRAKK
CRACKLESPACKLE HOTPUNCTURE SPREADBURST
EYE TIME BUILDS PAST LIE
HOTPUNCTURES DRIES TO PYRAMID (silverimage of the sun
                sparkling chrome image of the sungod)

              PLACE OF PEACE

WORSHIP THE SUN IN TIME
WORSHIP THE SUN OUTSIDE TIME

WORSHIP THE SUN WITH NO TIME
WORSHIP THE TIMELESS SUN
THE SUN IS THE BEING OF FIRE AND HEAT
THE SUN IS THE CHANGER OF ENERGIES
THE SUN IS THE GOLDEN MUSIC
THE SUN IS BRIGHT HOT AND FREE
THE SUN BURNS US BLACK AND GORGEOUS FOREVER
THE SUN IS OURSELVES THE SUN IS OUR SELVES THE SUN IS OUR SOULFUL BLACK SELVES.
THE SUN IS THE BEING OF FIRE AND HEAT
ALL ENERGY COMES FROM THE SUN
SUN OF GOD
SOULS OF GODFULL SUNS
SONS OF THE DEEPNESS IN US
DEEPNESS OF ALL BEING ALL OF THE FOREVER ALL OF THE SPACE
I AM USING ALL OF THE SPACE ALL OF THE SPACE FILL THE SPACE ALL THE
SPACE MY VOICE IS NOT HEARD MY FLESH IS NOT SEEN IT IS ALL THE SAME
FLESHVOICEHEATRAY ALL THE SAME HOTCHOICE ALL THE FIRELIFE COMING
COMING ALL SUN COMING FIRE COMING BEING COMING SPURTING DRIBBLINGS
SPARKLINGS CRYINGS BELLING CHIMING CRYING SPACKLECRACKLEING
WHINING BEINGS HIGH BEINGS A BEING ONE BEING A SUN A SUN BURNING
WORSHIP THE ALL-MIGHTY SUN. THE SUN IS OUR GOD THE SUN IS THE GOD
THE SUN IS THE WORSHIPER HIMSELF.
I am the son . . . . . yahaaa ooooo yahaaaoooo deedeedeedee come ba cho
I am the son the black holiness the goodness yaaaahoooo yaaaaaaaaa
Wake me up in me seeing you you son touch the goldeness yaaaaahoooo
Yaaaahooooooo sun in me rising above the tininess the space is filled
listen to son burn through you burn you up burn you up burn you up
yaaaaaaaaa dir dir rummmmmmm rummmmm doo eee doooo eee doooo eeee gooooo

Worshiping the sun a brother makes these sounds this is the self
that points to nothing points to itself being hot
eyes of fire warm me
Listen to the brother yahhhoooooeeeeeeeayayayayayayayaya
The black brother doing his thing, Ima do my thing always
I'ma always do my thing who dont like it, you dont like it foooooo

dodododod foooo dont get together run a slackjoke crate. Didn't know
it was weusi apollo last sun being first sun being in ghana in a gold
benny heatin up magic to reuse space better. Ima do my space using
thing now, watch out cold stuff, heatin up heatin up look at him
can you diiiiiiiiiiigg it?? can you diiiiiiiiggggit can you
use space this way cracker, naw you cant, where's jb come out do yo
dance clean up space, watch out for that motherfuckin flag dude, can
you diiiiiiiiiweusi apollo thales inventin sidespace . . . beepadeep
in space creatin new waves sidespace inside a drop of energy creatin
bein the energy the creator the lion man the dancer

groodasa bam bam crazy jump a dooby the rammer cut him cut out
icame back bleedin cape and shit hammer and shit horse and shit
standin in the san' a natural man bad as bad could be ima bad dude
anyway see my gold hat and hundred books and a staple of dudes spell
any shit you want bam bam bam bam slook at mchoro mweusi allah be
praised he dance. look clean up space clean up bam worshiping the
heavy self of fire. worshiping the heavy being of warmth and light.
was there was there was burning burn
ooooo came back see your mouth working
work out work out
slid got up from splittin split for days
here come beauty beauty here come beauty
here go here go look dig
yehhhh
yehhhh
worshiping the sun the sun
the fire worship the fire
worship the fire
the invisible always burning fire
the invisible always burning fire
the cracklespackle firebursts thunder lightning niggers
worship niggers
worship niggers
niggers should worship suns should worship the heat of blackness
as it turns you soul it turns you black its black beating heat out
you heatin up the world
heat up you heating heat up you heatin heat up heat heat heat
nigger worshiping blackness is blackness
space blackness waaaayyyyy dig it dig it yeh
waayyyyyy space blackness nigger worship space sun is god
sun is god waaayyyyyyy space blackness

/ 207

blackness
blackness
blackness
blackness
blackness
blackness   yeaaaaaaaaaaaaaaaaaaa's god

COME SEE ABOUT ME

OAllah
all deity, jinn, spirit creation
on the earth, where we live, cut off from
righteousness
by devil
in corporated
come see about
we
us
black people your first creationsssss
all deity
hey god
spirit,
interior animation of existence
we here
cut off
in a devil land
we need something to be strong god
all spirit flesh us with strength to
allah give us will to
get up
and split
cut out a here
uhhuh
uhhuh
uhhuh
please great black creator
let us get our hat, from the ugly thing got us
let us, oh, allah, please, move from where
we at

Into ourselves into ourselves, where
into ourselves, into ourselves
digit
pleasure boat of sweet black memory
s where
anywhere the whole being is
anywhere the total vibration.

uhuh
uhhuh
aaaaaaaaahhuuhh
doodoo doo
doodoo doo

on into light with pharoah junior
on into our self my man and sweet lady
cool world around you
dig yourself

uhhuh
uhhuh
into ourselves 'swhere
to
involve
then
evolve,
                  yeh, gone

ALL IN THE STREET

Can you Imagine something other
than what you
see Something
Big Big & Black
Purple yellow
Red & green (but Big, Big & Black)
Something look like a city
like a Sun Island gold-noon
Flame emptied out of heaven
grown swollen in the center
of the earth
Can you imagine who would live
there
with gold streets
striped circled inlaid
with pageants of the rulers
victories . . . Imagine these streets
along which walk some people
some evolved humans
look like *you*
maybe walk, stroll
rap like you
sound like you
but maybe a lil difference
maybe different clothes
hip mighta changed
a lil, but they shoes still glow
black and brown mirrors for things
in the street
to dig themselves

Mounds of round sounds bubblin and bumpin
right out the ground
can dig it . . .uh?
can see it . . . uh?
can feel it . . . uh?
can be it . . . huh?
This is now-past what you touch today
can change black man behaving under
your touch the way you want it to.

Can you dig it . . . uh?
See, feel, touch, be
it, uh?

The homes like domes high sparkling pyramids
New red sphinx buildings, cat buildings
Sun buildings, star buildings, the teaching
of invisible beings . . . who we are is
The Magic People . . . The Black Genius
Prophets of the Planet . . . Look at
the clothes on the women the
beautiful sisters clothed in supernew
silk looking spun diamond lace
the geles and bubas of a future generation
as they sail across the city on their
way out rugs . . . way out waaaay
out way way out, and past the disease
of the cracker ruled present, when
we are men and women again
freed from the serpent's dung

Hear each other miles apart (without no telephones)
"Love I hear you from way cross the
sea . . . in East Africa . . . Arabia . . .
Reconstructing the grace of our
long past—I hear you love
whisper at the soft air as it bathes
you—I hear and see you"

"I hear and see you too brother Jones
from the year 1968 talking to me,
My long departed ancestor
The sounds and images are here where
you left them. All for us"

Time space manifest into the unity of
the creator. The Creator has all experiences
and we live as flying images of
endless imagination. Listen to the creator
speak in me now. Listen, these words
are part of God's thing. I am a
vessel, a black priest interpreting
the present & future for my people

Olorun— Allah speaks in and
thru me now . . . He begs me to
pray for you—as I am doing—He
bids me have you submit to
the energy.

He bids me pray that you submit
to the energy . . . the energy the energy the energy

The energy The energy the energy the rays
of God roared thru us all . . . uh
rays of God plunged thru us all-uh
bids me raise myself to tell you

Look!
Listen!
I am in an ecstasy a swoon in
actual touch with everything

These future rulers
are black
I see & hear them
now
I am in touch
w/ them. They speak and
beckon to me
Listen they speak thru
my mouth
"Come on—
"Come on—
"Come on—
"Come on—
  Come on—"
"Come on—"
They are in the energy
They have created, through their consciousness
a closer connection
w/ the energy
They speak thru
my mouth
"Come on—
"Come on—
"Come on—
"Come on—

Come on—"
on their way out rugs in silken garments
no cold can penetrate
They speak and beckon at you all
thru me now, as ancestors
We are the ancestors of
these black builders
and conquerors
They would appear right here to
say these things but do not want to
frighten you
instead
they speak thru
me
They say—"All Praise Black Fathers
& Mothers We know the struggle
you go thru now.
We know how hard it is to be black
in that primitive age. But do not
naaw . . . do not ever despair

We Won
We Here
We still fast and grooving
We still baddest thing on the planet
We still gentle hummers and oobeedah scatters
                          oobbbeeoobbee dah
                          oobbbeeoobbee dah
dah
dah
daaaah daaah oooobee obbee dah
Do not despair Ancient People
We are your children
and we have conquered
This is your blessing
and This is your reward
Do not despair gentle ancient
groovy ancestors.
We have conquered
and we await the rich legacy
of hard won blackness
which you create to leave
us

here in the black fast future
here among the spiritual creations
of natural man
Do not despair ancient Fathers and
Mothers there in old America
We are here
awaiting your gorgeous
Legacy. . . . .
          Here the contact is broken. . . .

JIM BROWN ON THE SCREEN

is the past in a new package, in daylight sunlight
with the white woman of his savagery done up in brown
for advertising newness in the deadness and liveness
in the oldness, of punctured, rotting, maggot loving A
merica. America. America, my cunt
tree
what an odd arrangement
of nature, a
cunt
tree
where the "one eyed bird" rules inside the heads of drylipped
slobberers
worshiping the blackwhiteness
of died Ann
Dyed Ann
who they killed anyway and shotup with their bulletejaculation
Dyed Annnnnnnnn who-muh they chang-ed into "dem"
tho she has a sheen of black beneath and makes her anyway more
than they could ever hope to imagine even on the silver screek.
Jim Brown socked them. Socittoembabeeee
He knocked them down. Yea. Bad dude bad dude you dig him crack
that faggot in the mouth ... yeh (hand slap) 'sa bad motofreaky
Jim Brown put his hand on a white woman ... youmember he put his
hand on that gray bitch ... the one with ... yeh hell yeh, too much
oh man they doin that all overnow ... Poitier kissed one in the
mirror ... wat about that time Jimmy Brown kicked that sucker in
the nuts ... (hand slap) yeh ... yeh, knocked that motherfucker out

... in the space freakout station of our slavery
      mourn for us soldout and chained to devilpictures
          in this cold ass land of ruling doodoo birds and hairy ladies

I mean we walk in whiteness like the rest life sucked out on a
humble death eminent planned by whiteness to the white resolution
of all things. Jim Brown. Our man in space correcting the image
for now, with the old chain of whiteness forever, whiteness, for
ever, if he could escape, if he, could kill them all Jim, killem
Jim if he could, if he could race past any of them, again, like
he used to, in the real world, that image for us to build, among

the easy slickness of imitation, and accommodation. We know you livin
good Jim, we know you walk in stores and buy shit, (hand
slap, stomp, wheel) Yeh, we know you know all kinda hip folks
and talk easy in leather bars, and sashay through parties with
the eyes of our women and beastwomen glued to yo thang, Jim
you can be more than that anyway, more than a new amos in space
more than uncle thomas from inner plantation psychotic
cotton salvation you could be a man, Jim, our man on the land
our new creator and leader, if you would just do it and be it
in the real world
in the new world of yo own black people
I hope you do
it, Jim
I hope you unmaniquin yo
self, you can
do it, if you
want it, you can

you
sho
can, jim

LOVE IS THE PRESENCE OF NO ENEMY

In a blue summer ending begging of evening
a sum of blues endings aaaahhhs in harmony love knows
women walking
elbow triangles after the lost son
moon coming
the streets voice warm and sliding simmering snaky blues
evening
joy to be
too warm and moving
stop and hit that note
wave at the women
talk to the men
somewhere to go
building something
lights on all night
warm summer air niggers voices
they wearing long dresses and meticulous african hair

waves in the evening
soft voice chanting
purple in the air where the colored folks
live
aaah so lovely to be
free of ugly-nature
free of death and greed
rising expanding to be the father of Ras
and Obalaji
husband
to the beautiful
Amina
all the world inhales, in its blue perfection

Monday a devil will try to judge me, and fail
my eyes will burn through his brain and in the hollow of his head
maggots will boogaloo in death the celebration of new ideas of new issues
to come, and the judge will not understand
in his mumbling lip shuffle, he will cough and fire will eat his mistakes
he will look away, and try to remember who he is
and reeds of the new world will sway grown tight around him

and the beauty of tale of confrontation (sometime later, at that moment,
little black princes trading talk in future places know the finality
of this low thing's defeat at the hands of Maulana the warrior
who slew devils in their clawed gore, so that we might live
in better ways than catholics or jews or protestants or democrats
or republicans or white panthers or trotskyites or "humanists" or
any freaky connector with the dead scale and measure
so that we might rise so high a whole other thing will have to be
to contain us, and then, as the righteous, the soulful, the creative,
the just, the flaming, and then, as men, as rulers, as lovers of the
infinite truth.

play on play on in the warm blue road
know you doin it. Cant get far from indigo whispers.
Our love is here its grown so full. Our hearts from Be have
become what they must be. Be. we say, for the coming revelation. BE
we say, as the black hearted revolutionaries. BE, we say to the epoch of
tomorrow. And tomorrow is now. And Now is when we mean.

BAD NEWS FOR YOUR HIGHNESS (Song to Deposed Kings)

Slobber pave feet. Blow sun
nig los agin pick down foot
cop again, arm bandit faster
nigger close to dead, and
mama close to dead, italian
money makin machine nigger &
his dopey queen sit on a stoop
wait for biscuit to blow um down.
dope in a arm. The sun.
dope in a leg. The warm water from heaven.
dope in a brain. The collection of beauty reprises itself.
dope in the ground dope in the sound of the beating of the earth's heart.
flow dope swifter than words or deeps
flow italian money from street to street in the arms and hearts of my people
who love you italians
who like you to have rugs in yr cellars
and rugs in your bathroom while they have no covering even on their assholes
flow italian dope in the white hatted little pimplefaced fag who brings it
flow italian dope in the arm and lipstick of the pope who brings it too
may you all O.D. together like my people, my brothers down the street, who like
to O.D. they do it all the time

why is dope so nice to us why do we like it
why is highness so nice why do we allways be it
dope is shit shit eater put shit in yr arm in yr mama's tears
when they drag you out a hallway, and sheldon boloney giggles about it

what difference do it make, stay high, sucker chump, layout and be cool
the devil is corny, we know that, aint that the secret, brother, the cool
ness, the whole of elijah digested under your sky, kneeling in a hallway
slowmotion fastmotion blood congealed on the dropper fire swoopin up your
throat, last minute regrets, shit took you off, sheldon boloney gigglin

220 /

SOMEBODY'S SLOW IS ANOTHER BODY'S FAST   (PREACHMENT)

Somebody's slow is another body's fast
how fast we gon travel, to get up outta here
how fast can we move to move on way from this jive
how quick can we slick, how quick can we untrick
our slick self, dazzled by devils, shining weights
on our knees, tricks is good, say a trick, nick, he'sa hip kid
sells his mama's children dope for a green vine, cool in hell, cool
cool cool. Somebody's fast is no food at all, stalled on the lowway
with all our toll gol ripped off by unconscious pieces of our self.
My heart, my love, my shriveled mind, my eye, my touch, my feeling, all
hurdle and float, they out on the block, they on different sides of the
street. On different sides of the question, "allahu akbar" over here, right
on" over there, "habari gani" all up in around where i am, and we still, all
of us, somebody's slow stool for muddy feet. The bloody foot-claws
of a beast, squash our naked brain. Blood, and mud, mix with brown gray
brain meat. The sparks droop, the fire wilts, mud images and blood
images. Yusef says we are frankenstein dancing to the music of a Mad
soulless beast. But its our music. Its our rhythm. Its our sound and fury.
We hip and fast. We travel without touchin the ground. Dig me Dig me
Dig me. We say. But thats all we say. Dig me Dig me its a putt putt sound
to DraculaPig teeth ripping black sky's blood. On the way to cool moon
Dracula Pig teeth on the way to cooooool mooooooon. We gotta get faster
if fast will do it. We gotta be slicker if slick gonna get it. Here's
a slick trick to us in a green cadillac a green hat a green suit a green
finger nail file and green dirt underneath green finger nails. He's green
and hes mean clean as somebody humping his mama for 300 years can sell it
to you sell it to you buy it nigger buy it, can sell or give or make you
believe anything. I'm god up here on the wall. Dumb ass nigger. I'm super
smart having created even you from a higher form of life the african which
you now hate . . . . . heheheheheheheheheheheheh . . . can you understand . . . . .
a higher form of life . . . heh heh heh heh heh . . . . .
We are fast alright.
We better fast . . . lay off hogknuckles stuffed with cocaine and whitemagic
Lay off savages' flute farts for loud silence to cool the fool slave
Cool The Fool Slave. Give him job. Here. Give him white lady. Here.
Give him ideology. Here. Give him magic hatred of everything strong in
him. Here. Cool The Fool Slave. Here Monkey, jump up and down. Ok throw
fist up in air, say power to the people. Here. Good. Ja wohl my man.
Ok all those who don't want to get shot straight out just crawl up
in visionary bedrooms with negative aspects of the shadow and call our

name every five seconds till you change. Here. Every Five Seconds.
God. Jesus. Darwin. Marx. Marcuse. Here. Whhhh Whhhh Whhhh Whhh Whhh
Yes. Whhhhh. Right. Whhhhh. On Whhhhhh
Yeh (nods, droops, scratches) Yeh. Whhhh. (Snorts.)

We are very slow. See. Very slow. Get up.
We are not moving. I want warmth. Heat me. Get up. See. Move. Very
slow. Go faster. We are in our hip terribleness so cool yet slow.
A rocket bursts past our face killing our whole history.
The sphinx our father squats in the desert waiting to be caught up with.
We are very slow, he says. Unmoving to make us dig ourselves.
Pharoah, listen to Jr. Walker. Jr. Walker. listen to the silence of the
desert. James Brown read Mwalimu Nyerere. Staple Singers read A Black
Value System. We are very slow. Listen. A breath, murmur ancient one
hum pick up rhythm rock a ceiling of sun our selves rising birth.
Are we alive
Yes. But we are barely moving. Too slow. Go head brother move.

Go ahead me you. Be us.
Head speak to hand. Leg respond. I love. Feel
Ohhhh. Feel. Here I am
Touch me. Pull it all in hear. Hear.
I weeee. Bee Weeee. A weeeeee. Us need. Us. Us need. our self's. Us
cd be, big as sea, big as we, we big, we love. Feel. Head know eye.
Eye. See. Ear. Hear. Hand, what you doing. Doing. Are you doing. That's
njema, hand. Call foot mouth, tell him to pick up. Call heart to pump
food to fist. Yeabo. Move. That's hip, njema. Njema. Hofu ni kwenu, we
whisper along the veins of black existence. Hofu ni kwenu, along all
beautifuling chords of black life, my fear, my love, my fear, is for
you, us, we us, only i to make black, weusi, njema, hofu ni kwenu . . .
a call like the wonderful ripples of eternal water, carrying the touching
of mungu roho, holyspirit, can the outside reach the inside, holy consci
ousness, can the sidewalk, talk to the black ghost of love. Vibration
soft thunder, jagged edge of always terrible perfection, touch touch,
speak pamoja, unison. One word. One sound. One final, never always, its
not is, the one, ooooooo, alll, the circle, what, see, see, you can we
are, the bee, the beee, to beee, the all, the alll, ooooooooo, spirit
spirit spirit spirit . . . . .
And what is left is moving constant tremble lifes alive
Can we raise ourselves. Increase the vibration. The cycle of life to
constant frequency.

All is
none is
constant.
It is all vibration
The swing of endless pendulum
I want we.
We as the two extremes oned.
Atone.
A Z one strike forever moving claaaaaaaaaaaaaaannnnnnnnnnnggg
Clang in us
A Z oned atone.
We are a man meditating. We are bodies moving together in love.
We are communities looking into the sky for a moment on the clear way
to liberation. We are cities readying brothers to lead us. We are
nation, great body, collect the fragments of the milky way, aswirl
atop our heads, where thru the cosmic voice like perfect jagged steel
stabs in stabs in the be
the be
and we
will be

KUTOA UMOJA

oooowwoooooooooo what can it be
what can it beeee owooo woo bee
what can it beeee eeeee eeee eooooooooooo
thats holdin me
what can it beeeee eeeee
thats holdin
holdin
me
holdin
me,
from
from
gettin
freee
owwooooo owooooo do you do you knoooooooooooo
if you do
tell me tell me tell me owwooooo you don know
maybe its just we always talkin mememememe
when its wewewewewewe
its that mmeee mmmeeee
its that me thats holdin we
we need to hook all them meeeeeeeeeeees
togethetha
all them bad bad meeeeeees
together
close close
together
all them muslims, methodists, panthers, nationalists, jitterbugs
pimps, hooked up sweetfleshd mamas, all usyallthem insideourselves
need to get on out side ourselves . . . . . all them meeeeees need to
hook up into a big we a big we
a big big black black weeeeeee
all them big black bad bad meeeees
need need needta hook up hookhook hook up
in a bad black wee a bad badd a black black black
we
yeh
a bad weee
yeh yeh
a bad bad wee see yeh wee a wee a bad bad black
devil jammin we
yeh

THE SPIRIT OF CREATION IS BLACKNESS

Whatever happens we know we've lived
continue stream of fire, zagged airburn
showup baby you me a star, get together with
the purest magnetism. We are sons drawing new life
go, together, as part of the same. Inside outside, burn
the same, dawn, sunset, climb a rope robed animal disappear
the same. Scramble up the pyramid. Hallelujah among the pyramids.
Preach an scream and dance atop the pyramid. Salute yr father the sphinx
His lions legs and bulls body. His African patience to cool it so long
out in the sand, to teach a bunch of ovyo bloods wandering around the world.
But what ever's gonna happen its happening. Look hand fist a torch shoved
above our head. And we can see. The way we moved drawn on by our selves
hot looks. The heads a projector please turn it to fast motion smiling so
silent in the dark amidst the images, when they come out they melt the snow
show us where to go and we on the road already, we are our roads you know
Your brain cd catch your head on fire and it skeet fire like on a weird
calendar around yr television knot. Itd be screaming look dig this
something outside about to spring, and you better come warm yourself by my
screamin knot. You never seen nobody cd walk around with they haid on fire
and still sing the blues. But these are the reds, the greens the holy blacks
of the necessary harmony. And theyd come all those who survived the snows
cd hear or see or feel the umchababy sizz thru um, wd turn from the bullshit
they was doing and stumble, move on over to where we was campin out in motion
like the emotional erector set of flesh and spirit. Institutions of Blackness
Anti Slavery brigade blowin hot changes for the advertised season comin comin
And they'd come, bea bunch, a nation of em, yo head, our head be burnin
so bad be burnin so good, wd light up where we was the world cd see and blind
niggers be visionary blackmen rightaway and walk across their watery chains
reconstruct their whited out brains, and do the rhythmpop slow in fast motion glistenin
like the jewelry they digs, shine out like the hippopotamus topped alligator
wheeled Funkmobiles they invented, for the movements sake, for the sounds
sake, for the screech and tiptoes sake, for the colors sake, for the
ahhaaahahahahahahaha's sake, and the yehman's sake, and digit's sake
and the yougotit's sake, and the youthinkso huh's sake, and the
sake of the shadow that drags along envying the body of the blood he longs
to climb into unity with us and our father the son who art in the safe
and peaceful place. (We lean across the space of meeting, say yeh, go head
do what you gotta do. its alright. the sun come up, most likely . . . and
everything'll be all right . . . .
Yo head be all our heads and its risen like it was the sun drawn you up
with it, and we are drawn around in tune like motion, plane you plane me
are plane we, a crowd of us, swahili black, weusi jua, and there are words

/ 225

with this melody, and words and melody, tune, rhythm, the harmony, are all the same.

we merge with it
all things are it
we rhythm and sound and suncolor
we rise and set and sing and move
oh lord, oh lord, oh lord . . . . . .

SNAPSHOTS OF EVERYTHING

We are picked, and pick ourselves, for what we do and are
We make our eyes stretch and fill our bones, pack our heads
with what we want to pack them with, then look for a road
and that looking is itself a road, then we walk our walk
and talk our talk, all of it together, creating the thing
we are.
If we are something we can love, laughter is edens rain
our work good work love builds it dirt and hope and flowers
of thought. Reach and climb into talking pictures ourselves we puton like
warm flesh garments. Snug up the mind so the brain fits, so the words
come out right. In the darkness we stare at our brothers performing are we growing
our way. We walk our road and look at the sights we are sights for other travelers
What do they see, in what kind of album, and does it matter.

Going to the common paradise, men and women children and all the other stuff we need
for a really good rime. Its rhythm that carries us anyway. The beat reality's
heart. And what we are is gestures of the master, without space without time, dont put us
 down
as merely singers, we are the song

AFRIKAN REVOLUTION

AFRIKAN REVOLUTION

(Conakry, Guinea, February 4, 1973
after Amilcar Cabral's funeral)

Afrikan People all over the world
Suffering from white domination
Afrikan People all over the world
Trying to liberate their Afrikan nation(s)
Afrikan People all over the world
Under the yoke, the gun, the hammer, the lash
Afrikan People all over the world
being killed & stifled melted down for the Imperialists cash
Afrikan People all over the world
   conscious, unconscious, struggling, sleeping
resisting, tomming, killing the enemy killing each other
Being hurt, surviving, understanding, held in ignorance
Bursting out of chains, lying for Nixon, drowning colonialists
Being shot down in the street
Afrikan People everywhere
Afrikan People all over the world
Evolving because of & in spite of ourselves
Afrikan People all over the world, trying to make Revolution
The world must be changed, split open & changed
All poverty sickness ignorance racism must be eradicated
Who ever pushes these plagues, them also must be eradicated
All capitalists, racists, liars, Imperialists, All who can not change
they also must be eradicated, their life style, philosophies
habits, flunkies, pleasures, wiped out—eliminated
The world must be changed, split open & changed
Transformed, turned upside down.
No more Poverty!
No more dirty ragged black people, cept from hard work
   to beautify + energize a world we help create
Death to Backward Powers
Death to Bad Dancers
   No more trash piled up in the streets
   No more wind in the bedroom
No more Capitalists in penthouses & colored people in tents
   with no houses
Death to disease & carriers of disease
All disease must be cured!

"Individuals" who love disease must be reeducated
If they resist world unity and the progress of all races
Kill them. Don't hesitate! Kill them. They are the Plague
No more filthy places for us to live and be uneducated
No more aimless black children with nothing to do, but die
Death to the creators of unemployment
What do they do for a living? They are thieves.
Jail them! Nixon is a sick thief why does he
remain alive? Who is in charge of killing him?
Why is it Cabral, Lumumba, Nkrumah, Moumie,
Malcolm, Dr. King, Mondlane, Mark Essex, all can
be killed by criminals, & the criminals are not
hung from bridges? No more unfair societies!
We are for world progress. Be conscious of your
life! We need food. We need homes; good
housing—not shacks. Let only people who want to
live in roach gyms live in roach gyms
We do not want to live with roaches. Let
Nixon live with roaches if he wants to. He
is closer to a roach. What is the difference
between Nixon and a roach?
Death to bad housing
Death to no work
We need work. We need education so
we can build houses and create work for
ourselves. All over the world we Afrikans
need to make progress. Why do Europeans
Why do white people why do ignorant
people of our own race obstruct us.
STOP OBSTRUCTING US EUROPEANS!
STOP OBSTRUCTING US IGNORANT PEOPLE OF
   OUR OWN RACE
   Niggers, NeoColonized Amos + Andies
   Everywhere in the Afrikan World.
No more traitors! Death to traitors
   Dope Pushers should be killed
   Niggers who inform on Revolutionary Movements
   Should be killed
   Assassins masquerading as heroes
   Butlers masquerading as presidents of

  Afrikan, & Asian & South American
  Nations. They have made them Dough-Nations
So the superpowers can make they bread.
 Leaders who want dialogue with South Afrika
 Leaders who want to box in South Afrika
 Leaders who want to sing in South Afrika
 Leaders who want to observe South Afrika
These are not Leaders but Pleaders and
they should be beaten till their yoke and
their white are stiff & exposed
No more useless pain
We must refuse to be sold out by anyone
The world can be changed, we do not have to lick
 the pavements
All over the world the world can be changed
No more stupid ugliness everywhere
Death to the vultures of primitive disease +
 ignorance, America must change or be
 destroyed. Europe must change or be
 destroyed. Capitalism must be destroyed.
 Imperialism will die. Empty headed
 mummified niggers who support racist
 rule over black people will be killed too.
 Dope peddlers, Pimps, Teachers who teach
 Europe's lies, Doctor's who love money more
 than people, muggers, pretenders of revolution,
 Sterile intellectuals, Soul singers who
 Sold their soul to the soulless—live people who live
 their lives for the dead—all—change or die!
The world revolution cannot be stopped. Understand the
new criteria of life or forfeit what little life you have.
We will not be poor any longer
We will not be dirty, or ashamed of ourselves
 Racists, Capitalists, Imperialists, Sick People
 Fascists, racist rulers of Black,
 Lovers of disease, change or die
 Oppressed People of the world change
 or die
 Afrikan People. all over the world Rise
 & Shine
 Shine
 Shine

Afrikan People all over the world, the future is ours
We will create on our feet not our knees
It is a future of Great works, and Freedom
But we can not crawl through life drunk &
unconscious we cannot dance through life
or read the NYTimes through life, or wear vests
all of our life give our lives to parties, & work with no
reason but life in a prison of white domination,
Be conscious. Black People
    Negroes
    Colored People
    Afro Americans Be
    CONSCIOUS
You know you can run your own life
You can have all the money & food & good life
you need
    Be conscious
    meet once a week
Meet once a week. Talk about how to get
    more money, how to get educated, how
    to have scientists for children rather than
    junkies. How to kill the roaches. How to
    stop the toilet from stinking. How to get a
    better job. Once a week. Start NOW.
    How to dress better. How to read.
    How to live longer. How to be respected
    Meet once a week. Once a week.

All Over the world. We need to meet once a
    week. All over the world Afrikans, Soul
    Brothers Good Sisters we need to meet.
How to live longer be healthier build houses
run cities understand life be happier
Need to meet once a week
OK All over the world
Once a week
All over the world Afrikans
Sweet Beautiful Afrikans
NewArk Afrikans (Niggers too)
Harlem Afrikans (or Spooks)
Ghana Afrikans (Bloods)
Los Angeles Afrikans (Brothers)

Afrikan Afrikans (Ndugu)
West Indian Afrikans (Hey man)
South American Afrikans (Hermano!)
Francophone Afrikans (Monsieur)
Anglophone Afrikans (Mister Man)
Anywhere Afrikans
Afrikans Afrikans Afrikans
People
Afrikans Afrikans Afrikans
Watu Wazuri
Afrikans all over the world
Moving to the new way
A world of Good people is coming!
We gonna help make that world
We gonna help eliminate the negative
accentuate the positive
yellow folks brown folks red
folks will too
they hurting
I can't speak for white folks, they'll
speak for themselves
But the rest of us, Everybody Everybody
Everybody, let us first deal with us
Afrikans
All over the world, Yes, Everywhere Everywhere
Everywhere, we are Afrikans
& going to make change
Change or die
Afrikans
Change or die
to the Whole world too
we are Afrikans
Love is our passport to the perfectability of humanity
Work & Study
Struggle & Victory

HARD FACTS

INTRODUCTION

POETRY IS SAYING SOMETHING ABOUT REALITY. IT REFLECTS THE SAYER'S PLACE IN THE production process, his or her material life and values. As a form, it reflects the material life and values of the society in which it exists. And in which the sayer, the poet, exists.

The various trick definitions of poetry and its uses, whatever they are, no matter how "deep," profound, obtuse, obvious, irrational, etc. reflect exactly a specific group of people and a specific production and social relationship of that group to the society in which they live and to the world.

For instance, the middle-class poetry which is most important to the American Academy is a reflection of American middle class life and interests, petty bourgeois social and production relations. The White middle class—the Black middle class, finally, after some conflict about national oppression *can* curve into a single curve, a diphthongated yet whole "strata" of material life & values—e.g., the poetry of Nikki Giovanni, quite energetic at one point in reflecting our national oppression, can very quickly settle into the class interests of the American bourgeoisie in general, because the material life and values though not as monied probably as Lowell or Rod McKuen, Mailer or Updike but we are an oppressed nation & our bourgeoisie is smaller, weaker, less powerful certainly than the main U.S. bourgeoisie, but they all we got! However, the interests, values and consciousness issue from a material base, absolutely supportive of, finally an "extension" of, the material base, interests, values & consciousness of the American ruling class. Poetry is apologia for one particular class or another and that class's views, needs and visions.

The poetry, art or writing reveals the class stand, and attitude of the writer, reveals the audience to whom the writer and artist address themselves, it also reveals what work they have been active in and what studies they are involved in. There is no art that is above the views or needs or ideology of one particular class or another, tho the rulers pretend that art is classless and beyond political definition. That is why we aim at an art that serves the great majority of people, the working masses of people. That is why we make an art that praises what helps the people and puts down mercilessly what oppresses or exploits them. That is why we should try to make a poetry, an art that speaks to, *after 1st learning from,* those same dynamic working masses. We learn from the omnieyed, multinational mass, the scattered, raw, unsystematized, and even refined, and reorganize re-intensify, dynamize, make gigantic and give back what we have learned. We deal with reality, "to get truth from facts," as Mao says, and with the class stand, attitude and strength of the inspired worker give it back to inspire, educate, mobilize, persuade, involve, the people. We want to raise the level of the people, but to do that we must start where they are which is on a much higher level than the majority of intellectuals and artists. We also want to popularize, to make popular, to make a popular mass art. To take the popular and combine it with the advanced. Not to compromise, but to synthesize. To raise and to popularize.

The question of the audience is key, is central to the work. "For Whom" is the problem as Mao Tse-tung sounded it. For whom does one write, the audience standing there as you compose, to whom, for whom, it is directed. That is the key to the class stand and attitude of the work. That answers the question of whether or not the art serves the people or serves their exploiters. If we address our work to a small circle of the hip urban middle class, the petty bourgeoisie who are the writers, intellectuals, finally that's who it will be for, and it will tend to be narrow and individualistic and not reflect the truly universal, the truly lasting, the truly modern, the truly good. And what about the artists and writers whose works aim for Rocky's living room as their legitimatizing focus or who see honorary membership in the Jet Set as hip when it is merely the flashy part of the class of vampires that control the world.

The work and study should be work, active work, toward making revolution, toward seeing the masses of people in this society 1st build a revolutionary vanguard party, a new communist party, an anti-revisionist party, a party guided by the science of Marxism-Leninism-Mao Tse-tung Thought, and then led by that party smash the bourgeois state machine and seize state power to turn the means of producing wealth, the land, factories, machines, mineral wealth, from private property owned by a handful of superbillionaires to state owned public property under the dictatorship of the proletariat. That is the work we are putting forth. The study should be of revolution as well as art. But revolution 1st, and foremost. Getting to know the people and letting them get to know you. Studying the world based on the science of Marxism-Leninism-Mao Tse-tung Thought. Because this will clarify and change your class stand from petty bourgeois to proletarian. From a sideline watcher of the struggle, to remold your worldview to that of the working class and the revolutionary. For whom: For the people, for the revolutionaries, but also for the generations to come reared under the dictatorship of the proletariat, socialism and communism.

Yes, poetry should be a weapon of revolutionary struggle. And we say it again. Otherwise it is "a teacup in Rocky's summer place," a distraction, an ornament the imperialists wear to make a gesture toward humanity.

But many of us feel since we are "anti-establishment" that that makes us heroes. Nonsense. Most such anti-establishmentarianism is just petty bourgeois anarchism and failure to take up the responsibility intellectuals had better understand they have to actually help make life better for all of us.

Also, the unclarity, romanticism, sadness, & pessimism, the little tearful odes to weakness we write. The people don't need these. They need odes of strength, attack pieces, bomb, machine gun and rocket poems. Poems describing reality and methods of changing it. Rhythmic reading lists, objectivity, clarity, information, science, as well as love and concern.

We should not act or write like we're crazy, but as impassioned revolutionaries aiming to help destroy the capitalist system! Be passionate, but disciplined enough to deliver the death blow! And we should be reading, discovering the world, through the classics, Marx, Engels, Lenin, Stalin, Mao, etc., working in it day to day in hard struggle against the enemies of humanity, otherwise what are we writing about—our last poem? We become old American academics reflecting on our gardens & the newest frog to croak there—even if the garden is Lower East Side or Fillmore, West Side, Europe, Afrika, sets & countersets, world exercises in smartness & compromise. It all becomes celebration of the power of the world's rulers and even their "liberalism" that can permit of people jumping out windows, screwing their grandmothers, or performing cunnilingus (what?) on the silver screen!

We need a poetry that directly describes the situation of the people and tells us how we change it. That shows us our lives and gives us the responsibility for mobilizing them around life and revolution rather than drifting impotently in support of death and bourgeois rule.

This is difficult because many poets, etc., in U.S. are petty bourgeois—i.e., the class that vacillates. Revolving like tops between bourgeois interests & consciousness & the interests & consciousness of the oppressed masses. The struggle to change that consciousness where it does not vacillate is a revolutionary struggle and it can only be achieved by struggling to change external reality! Earlier our own poems came from an enraptured patriotism that screamed against whites as the eternal enemies of Black people, as the sole cause of our disorder & oppression. The same subjective mystification led to mysticism, metaphysics, spookism, etc., rather than dealing with reality, as well as an ultimately reactionary nationalism that served no interests but our newly emerging Black bureaucratic elite and petty bourgeois, so that they would have control over their Black market. This is not to say revolutionary Black nationalism is not necessary, it was and is to the extent that we are still patriots, involved in the Black Liberation Movement, but we must also be revolutionaries who understand that our quest for our people's freedom can only be realized as the result of Socialist Revolution!

Our nationalism was reactionary when it focused on White people as the cause of our oppression rather than the system of monopoly capitalism. Perhaps the lack of struggle orientation that we observed among the White petty bourgeois arty types fueled our belief in racial analysis. But the reality is that we were reacting to petty bourgeois vacillation & uncommittedness to anything but individual hedonistic ease and the hip service of the bourgeoisie which we still oppose and aim to denounce!

All this + our own vision clearing, our own move toward clarity & reality. "It is a time of great disorder," says Mao. "A very good thing for the People." The oppressive systems shaking & wheezing, revolutionary forces, mobilizing & clarifying.

This is the period now after the defeat in Southeast Asia when the United States has been shaken as a world power, and is now in absolute contention with the Soviet Union, the other superpower, for control of the world, which neither will get. But this contention all over the world, under the disguise of detente will more than likely lead to war. All over the world as well, the people are opposing the superpowers, and all imperialism, and led by the forces of the Third World are making revolution and objectively building the world front against imperialism. In the U.S.A. it will mean that since the superprofits are being blown away ... that the workers and oppressed nationalities will no longer be able to be lulled with concessions or bribed or bourgeoisified, because the 6/10ths of 1% who rule this state will insist on their maximum profit and intensify police repression and go to fascism if they have to, to protect their maximum profit. That is why the cutbacks and layoffs and rising unemployment. In the next few years there will be an increasing attack on the revolutionaries in this country, characterized by the S-1 Bill and other attempts to legislate fascism, and it will be important for there to come into existence a united front of intellectuals and artists who can unite to fight against the enemies of a new life, the enemies of the people. Even though there would be disagreement in such a front, since all the progressive artists are not communists, we feel such a front, based on unity and struggle must come into existence! To unify around those essential tasks upon which we agree, perhaps, anti-imperialism, anti-racism, anti-capitalism, anti-women's oppression, the need for a new revolutionary art, perhaps we could put together a dynamic coalition of forces that would make the cultural revolution that was only halfmade in the 60's because it pulled up short with nationalism, even though it was correct in rejecting bourgeois ideology, and fleeing the castles of the bourgeoisie. But now it is a new day, it is time for a higher stronger art, a deeper more thoroughgoing and all sided commitment to the masses of humanity. It is time for the artists and writers and intellectuals in the U.S.A. to choose sides openly and fiercely and begin to struggle with no holds barred, to carry the revolution through to the end.

Also, a new revolutionary Marxist-Leninist party, a new instrument of people's struggle will soon be born. It will be constructed out of the concrete conditions of America today! All the fresh & fiery forces of history and commitment led by Blacks, Browns, Reds, Yellows & Whites. Led by the mass of workers & oppressed nationalities. A joint hammer of humanity raising to strike, to tear down the enemies of human life & development!

LONG LIVE REVOLUTIONARY ARTISTS & WRITERS!
MARXIST-LENINISTS UNITE—WIN THE ADVANCED TO COMMUNISM!
BUILD A REVOLUTIONARY MARXIST-LENINIST COMMUNIST PARTY!

LONG LIVE THE ANTI-IMPERIALIST CULTURAL UNION!
LIBERATION FOR THE BLACK NATION!!
SOCIALIST REVOLUTION!!!
VICTORY TO ALL OPPRESSED PEOPLE!!!!

—Amiri Baraka
October 1974–November 1975

REVOLUTIONARY LOVE

Black Revolutionary Woman
In love w/Revolution
Your man better be a revolution
for you to love him
Black Revolutionary woman
the care of the world
is yours, in your hands is
entrusted all the new beauty
created here on earth
Black revolutionary woman
were you my companion I'd
call you Amina, Afrikan faith
and inspiration, were
you my comrade in struggle, I'd still
call you lady, great lady
Bibi, Black Revolutionary Woman
were you my woman, and even in the pit
of raging struggle, we need what we love,
we need what we desire to create, were you
my woman, I'd call you companion, comrade,
sister, black lady, Afrikan faith, I'd call you
house, Black Revolutionary woman
I'd call you wife.

WATERGATE

"Dead Crow" is an ol ugly
eagle
i know
run a "eagle
laundry"
wash
eagles
over & over
this eagle wash
hisself
like lady macbeth
blood mad & sterile
hooked teeth
pulled
out
in a flag costume
just stripes
no stars

WHEN WE'LL WORSHIP JESUS

We'll worship Jesus
When jesus do
Somethin
When jesus blow up
the white house
or blast nixon down
when jesus turn out congress
or bust general motors to
yard bird motors
jesus we'll worship jesus
when jesus get down
when jesus get out his yellow lincoln
w/the built in cross stain glass
window & box w/black peoples
enemies we'll worship jesus when
he get bad enough to at least scare
somebody—cops not afraid
of jesus
pushers not afraid
of jesus, capitalists racists
imperialists not afraid
of jesus shit they makin money
off jesus
we'll worship jesus when mao
do, when toure does
when the cross replaces Nkrumah's
star
Jesus need to hurt some a our
enemies, then we'll check him
out, all that screaming and hollering
& wallering and moaning talkin bout
jesus, jesus, in a red
check velvet vine + 8 in. heels
jesus pinky finger
got a goose egg ruby
which actual bleeds
jesus at the apollo
doin splits and helpin
nixon trick niggers
jesus w/his one eyed self

tongue kissing johnny carson
up the behind
jesus need to be busted
jesus need to be thrown down and whipped
till something better happen
jesus aint did nothin for us
but kept us turned toward the
sky (him and his boy allah
too, need to be checkd
out!)
we'll worship jesus
when he get a boat load of ar-47s
and some dynamite
and blow up abernathy robotin
for gulf
jesus need to be busted
we ain't gonna worship nobody
but niggers gettin up off
the ground
not gon worship jesus
unless he just a tricked up
nigger somebody named
outside his race
need to worship yo self fo
you worship jesus
need to bust jesus (+ check
out his spooky brother
allah while you heavy
on the case
cause we ain gon worship jesus
we aint gon worship
jesus
we aint gon worship
jesus
not till he do somethin
not till he help us
not till the world get changed
and he ain, jesus ain, he cant change the world
we can change the world
we can struggle against the forces of backwardness, we can change the world
we can struggle against our selves, our slowness, our connection with
   the oppressor, the very cultural aggression which binds us to our enemies
   as their slaves,

we can change the world
we aint gonna worship jesus cause jesus dont exist
xcept in song and story except in ritual and dance, except in slum stained
tears or trillion dollar opulence stretching back in history, the history
of the oppression of the human mind
we worship the strength in us
we worship our selves
we worship the light in us
we worship the warmth in us
we worship the world
we worship the love in us
we worship our selves
we worship nature
we worship ourselves
we worship the life in us, and science, and knowledge, and transformation
of the visible world
but we aint gonna worship no jesus
we aint gonna legitimize the witches and devils and spooks and hobgoblins
the sensous lies of the rulers to keep us chained to fantasy and illusion
sing about life, not jesus
sing about revolution, not no jesus
stop singing about jesus,
sing about, creation, our creation, the life of the world and fantastic
nature how we struggle to transform it, but dont victimize our selves by
distorting the world
stop moanin about jesus, stop sweatin and cryin and stompin and dyin for jesus
unless thats the name of the army we building to force the land finally to
change hands. And lets not call that jesus, get a quick consensus, on that,
lets damn sure not call that black fire muscle no invisible psychic dungeon
no gentle vision strait jacket, lets call that peoples army, or wapenduzi or
    simba
wachanga, but we not gon call it jesus, and not gon worship jesus, throw
jesus out yr mind. Build the new world out of reality, and new vision
we come to find out what there is of the world
to understand what there is here in the world!
to visualize change, and force it.
we worship revolution

/ 245

NIGGY THE HO

Many years ago in ol time america
was a cherub culla gir name niggy
wanted to be a writer, sd she
cd dig the fire on the time, why
niggers ran in the street screamin
light as she was she sd she dug black
dig. She sd nigger can you kill which
remains a good question. can you indeed
once you dig what needs to be killed?
So she copped some heat from the rage
of the age, used some fire from the
ignited veins of the almighty spook.
I mean she did it, used it, laid it
somewhere and how, throwd it down,
some sd. But what was she sayin you
know what. what she put on paper the
limb of the body, a string on the
motion. like, you hadda have some notion
of what was going down. Hadda dig sumthin
even in a urban league machine. and they
create spooks ready for the press, clean
parts for the ominous rumbling turbines
of capital. They fits good, once they been
honed. They create em sometimes from ol
cornflakes meltin in the moonlight
missionary belches, racial squelches, a little
smoke, some blood, a few screams somewhere,
down the street, they hair stand on end, turn
half blond (some times) like civil rites,
and all the time merica wont let um have it
and they knew it was hip. Let em have it let em
have it let em have it, let em have it, klans
and lynchers, let em have it, roosevelts kennedys
dug what they really sd, let em have it klans &
lynchers let em have it, and so relented, yeh
they really understood. Ass the lady, whose lay
is she any way? CIA carry her little buttock cross
the see. Hi Ho, she in Dar, told them niggers
she rather be in nairobi, watchin kenyatta's teeth
turn to mud. Hi Ho, now she on the t.v.

wit you uncle bubba or your aunty jimmy
sayin open the rolls its time to cut the
jabber, i'm happy dont you know (read the
poem) & ready as come to go. Hi Ho, now she wit
the caucus, and the other eminent exploiters
of the race. Hi Ho, advice for the po, go
to yr local museum, give yo stomach growls a number
& try to sell em to the curator as conceptual art. HI HO,
Hi Ho, lincoln center crummy, wallow on yr tummy, gospel horror funky,
a mediocre flunky, now she say she really dig President Ford. Yahoo,
what else is new, Hi Ho, dont need to talk about killin no more
but nigger can you kill is still the theme, but now, Hi Ho, who need
killin, cause there's niggers needs it too, like a poetess lariot of
the world's exploiters. Hi Ho, her butt for sale everywhere, Hi Ho, ugly
American, sell out bitch scribbler, athletic supporter of imperialism,
all the perfume in the world cant cover the farts
of the maggots
in your
soul.

HISTORY ON WHEELS

Civil Rights
included Nathan
and the rest
of them, who got in america
big shotting off the agony
a class of blue Bloods, hip
to the swing and sway of
the usa. yeh all the 1st
negroes world wide, joined
knees, and shuffled heroically
into congress, city hall, the
anti-p program, and a thousand
penetrable traps of cookstove
america. a class of exploiters,
in black face, collaborators,
not puppets, pulling their own
strings, and ours too, in the
poor people's buck dance, w/o
the bux. But see, then later,
you talkin afrika, and its unity
like a giant fist of iron, smashing
"racialism," around the world. But see
that fist, any fist, reared back to
strike an enemy, shd strike the real
enemy. Not a colorless shadow for
black militants in residence, to
bloat the pockets and consolidate
the power of an international
bourgeoisie. In rag time, slanting
stick legs, with a pocket full of
toasted seaweed, and a bibliography
of bitter neocapitalists or bohemian
grays, celebrating life in a dark garage
w/all cars banned until the voodoo car
appear. The way the rich blackies showed
after we marched and built their material
base, now niggers are left in the middle
of the panafrikan highway, babbling about
eternal racism, and divine white supremacy
a hundred thousand dollar a year oppression

and now the intellectualization, the militant resource of the new class, its historical valorization. Between them, john johnson and elijah, david rockefeller rests his smiling head.

CLAY

Killed
by a white woman
on a subway
in 1964.
he rose
      to be the first negro congressman
      from missouri.
      we're not saying
      that being dead
      is the pre
      requisite
      for this honor
      but it certainly helped make him
      what he is
      today.

ROCKEFELLER IS YO VICE PRESIDENT, & YO MAMMA DONT WEAR NO DRAWERS

Kenny G. w/malla yalla (a fatlady /her own
circus) rounds the corner burping
for our people
               niggy g, the nongirl poet
               strokes Chakiris tool

            chas rangel, in drag, the new
            statue of liberty, he, and Shirl
            our lady of constant backwardness
whisper little nothings in gerald ford's ear
float out cross the airwaves for niggers to hear
the caucus, our new petitb, quislings already
in the new revolutionary years. Its just that we
got to build our systems of struggle, by struggling
with the ugliness in us, the guarded motion toward
the masters' life, the grim slavemaster capitalist
and the gruesome reactions to that which sometimes
are that, backwards, god in white face god in black
face, "protect our market" is a sign the priest and
poets union of south chicago raises instead of
ruthless struggle.
                  Oppressed nation rising in
          hook up with all the beat up peoples
          rising. Black workers, the masses of us
          in tune, with all workers, with all the strugglers
          focusing at last on concrete reality. We will organize
where we are, and make war on the enemies of humanity.

Dont be fantasizin bout no other jive
its time we sd it all and moved
its now its here its real check it close
describe reality and change it, build revolutionary
systems, and confront the beast clear
Seize the factories, land, sources of energy & state power
dictatorship of the builders, the workers, the whole
proletariat, black brown red yellow white, to
paralyze the instability of the multicolored middle class
+ crush by force
the resistance of the
bullshitters

TODAY

Reactionary middle class idealists
Forward wing of backwardness
Upside down intellectuals, with no base except
the barest form of groveling
Americana
niggers removed
from struggle
little
dabblers
Fellow travelers of
neo, semi &
full up
colonialism
misdefiners of reality
yr toilet bowl mentalities
must be flushed straight
away.
              Frustrated white boys
         screaming black to masquerade
      the fact you once used too much Nadinola
   before the Alabama Panther and Detroit
Red made Black Beautiful + potentially
powerful
organic food eating niggers
polygamous niggers
niggers w/feudalistic fantasies
cosmic niggers, niggers who think they militant
cause they dont eat spare ribs
niggers who think they revolutionaries
cause they hair aint combed
Skinny niggers taking 4 hours to prepare a special
Afrikan stu meanwhile regular
Black folks eat watermelons, okra, fried
chicken, turnips, all from
  Afrika
Abstract metaphysical shit talking bores
counter revolutionary, selfish, unserious pseudo
imitators, red baiters, poets forever in residence
Black studies pimps in interesting tweed jackets

Frauds in leopard skin, turbaned hustlers w/skin
type rackets, colored capitalists, negro
exploiters, Afro American Embassy gamers
who lurk about Afrikan embassies fightin for
airline tickets, reception guerillas, whose
only connection w/a party is the Frankie
Crocker kind.
Where is the revolution brothers & sisters?
Where is the mobilization of the masses led
by the advanced section of the working class?
Where is the unity criticism unity? The self criticism
& criticism? Where is the work & study? The
ideological clarity? Why only poses &
postures & subjective one sided non-theories
describing only yr petty bourgeois upbringing
Black saying might get you a lecture gig, "Wise
Man," but will not alone bring revolution.
Old time Afrika might be quaint "Black Giant"
But go live in the bush & throw bones
in the sand to tell time, dig a doodoo trench
chew a stick to clean yr teeth, & try to
bring food from the land, & you'll find out
what the people need! "Mama Malkia"
who want the 50 sisters for each brother
ancient hustler, yo loins long gone dont
have to serve, abstract atavistic theories to burden
our women w/idle nonsense. Maybe we
need to locate you a feudalistic paradise
hidden deep inside ovambo land wherein for
you to be anyhow wife no. 50! Down, lecture hall
hustler, on yr knees to grind the meal, wife 49
gonna check yr work out in a minute! Put a
note in a bottle, later on, let us check out
how it is. See if you can still run it on
our idealistic daughters, not clear on revolution.
All such hustlers, & rustlers, abstract elitists
con women, Alkebulan confidence mens,
Revolutionary Theory
Revolutionary Development

Revolutionary Party
Ends such parasitical life
to build a new world, in working build a
new person
new mind.

GIBSON

old boy in 1492, sailing west toward sun dash, was hip
we cd say what we wanted, you see, i never changed baby, never.
(in a hallway, lady mc, dragon lay, sips her sip a night)
i grew is what, i never never
changed. Angels zigzag on heads of pins. But black people still grin
when i show. I never
never
changed.
that year, 69, we worked to build our image among the
"militants"
sure enough, a little motion
from the rear
of the meeting
and i was in,
and the convention, i had bellbottoms
then, and 40 yng sisters
the gibson girls, swinging on
my charm.
i never, never
changed.
That campaign, when honey punched junius
in the snout
and i got my white technicians
down from
boston, to pull
the stuff
together. the business community
wasn't sure, I had some funny
friends, but, dig, i never, never
changed. Till bam, i beat him, and the
next election came, and wam, i mashed him,
and them dudes in the tall buildings
looked out, called out, sd, hey, ken, (dig?)
drop on in, get some dust, like get down,
and it all sailed, it got up, then, and sailed, away.
I'm over head, look up, a distant, blue bird, airplane, super-man!
till now, they march in front of my shop calling me names, them
same niggers I told how to make a mayor, them same crazy dudes
wit the afrikan names (they changed em?. talking that marx shit too . . . wow)
    But

I'm in shape, I jog around the park, I made my piece with the democrats
and they promised i cd get the nod for 80 in the congress, I travel all
over the world, japan, paris, west coast, i made a terrible speech about
the power was in the hands of the economic boys, and that yng kids shd
grow up to be the president of general motors
and not the mayor. Yeh.
and see, after congress, a cabinet post,
and the governor asks me, all kinds of things, calls me
daily, i go a lot of places with all the heavies, they need
my council, even Ford, when he got in, he called me first, you
see, and he's a lot straighter than mcgovern, them liberals, man,
is weak as water. power is where its at. give me power any time.
and newark? this town? why'd you ask, you can see it, cant you,
look out the window, there, just left of where that puerto rican bastard
bust out my new french glass, messed up my abstraction i got from
artie ruler, you say, you want to take a walk, hah, a walk, huh, through
newark, hah, you gotta be kiddin, wait, I'll call the police, i never
tho, never
never
changed.

REAL LIFE

Ted, Ted? In the bay at the bottom of the wat
er lies the president of the united states,
his chappaqui
dick, bent around an immigrant in an
automobile. Nixon calls from the coast, you thought
you'd get away clean, but my vengeance
comes from beyond the grave.
Nixon slobbers on the phone, wetting the cocaine on the desk
he and pat have been snorting since
early morning, herb alpert blurting low contradictions in the wings
Shadows gather on the windows, then blow twisted into the whole dark
which comes now. The lights go on
in the white house. Ford cracking his knuckles
turns off the tv and calls nixon
you alright dick, he says, white whistles jag at nixons calm, high
and wild, pat's jaws quivering, greens and blues come off the screen
and stutter 3-D in the room, sympathetic and wanting to rub them
he cant speak
rockefeller's talking
ford says the plan, was national
unity, the new money
and the old,
he cant speak, nixon cant, high, and hot, cripple forever upstairs
pat starts to pee on the rug, and roll in it. Her giggles like a vincent
price movie, without popcorn, nixon slobbers, trying to make a point, ford
is saying national unity, as rockefeller grins, his finger, shoving up into
the air, across a thousand miles, at the mad western capitalists and their
southern friends. Yall dont know how this shit works, he is saying (really)
the commentator, looks over his shoulder, as if he knows that nixon is
watching. Ford whispers numbly, dick, dick, yes,
mr. president?

RED AUTUMN

    communist sparrows gnawing on a fire escape
together in bread lines flying off to the next low house

    cant get up to prudential, that high white, w/the stain glass eyes
while indian summer flutters, drunks mutters, the little girl and i off to see

    her grand mother and father, and talk of the city's political corruption.
winter is yet ahead, we are readying to go to a women's conference and find ways

    to bring marxism-leninism-mao tse-tung thought to black women. Some sisters
pushing a proposal to call a multinational women's front together, by spring. Thats

    good, from the tactical to the strategic, build the whole structure that will
change the century, change the social system, change the way we live, change the peoples

    lives and the future of the world.

AT THE NATIONAL BLACK ASSEMBLY

"EEK

a nigger

communist," the lady democrat
nigrita squeeked, eek
an "avowed"
nigger
communist, & almost swooned
except you cd hear static chattering
from her gold necklace chairman
Strauss dialing trying to get through
her papers spilled
& the autographed picture
of Teddy K. & Georgie W.
hugging each other in
the steam bath
fell out.

You see she
say I cant not be
you see
with you niggers
with no nappy head commie
America's been good
to me. The democrats, God
bless' em, have alllllllways
done good
by us
by colored folks
you see she say I studied
commies, them chinese maoists
specially (She scooped her papers
up & thought deliciously
about the time her man
Scoop J & she licked on the same ice
cream
cone
right down to the hairs!

Specially them
Maoists, I studied
                They tacktix
She say, They tacktix
is to take over
the microphone &
be against the
democrats)
          sweeping out
           wrist radio tittering
          Strauss waltzes &
          Proposed ripoffs
          Straight from Watergate

Going to the airport
interviewed by WLIE
She smiled powdering her
conversation
  & caught a plane
   to
      petit bourgeois
            negro
                  heaven

3RD WORLD BLUES

Walk it slow
where you go
walk it slow
where you go
you want to know
you want to know
why its so
why its so
the world is black
the world is green
the world is red, yellow brown,
the world is mean
Walk it slow
you know its so
Walk it slow
you ought to know
Why its so
Why its so
We in the world
Poor as dirt
      Dont get some rhythm
Somebody'll get hurt
the world is black
the world is green
the world is red, yellow, brown
the world is mean

A NEW REALITY IS BETTER THAN A NEW MOVIE!

How will it go, crumbling earthquake, towering inferno, juggernaut, volcano, smashup, in reality, other than the feverish nearreal fantasy of the capitalist flunky film hacks tho they sense its reality breathing a quake inferno scar on their throat even snorts of 100% pure cocaine cant cancel the cold cut of impending death to this society. On all the screens of america, the joint blows up every hour and a half for two dollars an fifty cents. They have taken the niggers out to lunch, for a minute, made us partners (nigger charlie) or
surrogates (boss nigger) for their horror. But just as superafrikan mobutu cannot leop ardskinhat his
way out of responsibility for lumumba's death, nor even with his incredible billions rockefeller
cannot even save his pale ho's titties in the crushing weight of things as they really are. How will it go, does it reach you, getting up, sitting on the side of the bed, getting ready to go to work. Hypnotized by the machine, and the cement floor, the jungle treachery of trying
to survive with no money in a money world, of making the boss 100,000 for every 200 dollars
you get, and then having his brother get you for the rent, and if you want to buy the car you
helped build, your downpayment paid for it, the rest goes to buy his old lady a foam rubber
rhinestone set of boobies for special occasions when kissinger drunkenly fumbles with her blouse, forgetting himself.
If you dont like it, what you gonna do about it. That was the question we asked each other, &
still right regularly need to ask. You dont like it? Whatcha gonna do, about it??
The real terror of nature is humanity enraged, the true technicolor spectacle that hollywood
cant record. They cant even show you how you look when you go to work, or when you come back.
They cant even show you thinking or demanding the new socialist reality, its the ultimate tidal
wave. When all over the planet, men and women, with heat in their hands, demand that society
be planned to include the lives and self determination of all the people ever to live. That is the scalding scenario with a cast of just under two billion that they dare not even whisper. Its called, "We Want It All ... The Whole World!"

THE DICTATORSHIP OF THE PROLETARIAT

The dictatorship
of the proletariat
        you need to say that
          need to hear that
          not be scared of that
          cause thats gonna save your life
                gonna make your life life change from suffering

you hear that, the dictatorship
        of the proletariat, and be scared
        think somebody gonna hold you back
        hold you down, downer than you been held
        which aint even in it, is it. not downer than we been held cause
        we been held down, like down, down and dirty we been held, way down.

it shows you how powerful, how strong and cruel powerful
these capitalists are. these superbillionaire blood suckers
cause they put words in schools, radios, newspapers, televisions
words coming out of the heroic hero's mouth heroically. the happy cop,
the strong sensitive cop, the tall cop, the cop whose father wanted him to be a lawyer
and he's gonna make it one day type, the cop with the hip mustache, the laughing cop,
the hippy cop, batman and robin cops, nigger cops, negro cops, puerto rican patrolmen
all comin at you led by our loving goodguys from swat, just the thing for the superfly
all these herolover cops, are these the same which shoot yr little nephew in the back of the
head while he hanging up some crepe paper for a surprise birthday party down in the
   basement
where they got you living. Are these the same gentle goodguy heroes who killed the little
14 year old in bed stuy, the 12 year old in queens, the 18 year old in staten island, the
16 year old in long branch. the ones that slaughtered the 31 dudes in attica, and is that
the same attica where bald head mel stewart be sneakin cake to the inmates & they all
buddies grinning together and frankly happy they dont have to be out in the world
gettin in rich peoples way?

Yet when you hear the dictatorship of the proletariat. You dont know. You aint sure
You heard about hitler, and franco. The daily star ledger news courier times bulletin tells
   you dic
tatorship is bad. All but the dictatorship bein run now, the dictatorship of the minority
which is currently bein run, at this moment crushing yr whole self down, the one
mashin on you right now, is frankly, well listen to buckley, sammy davis, steinem,

/   263

woody allen, hip. newspeak for the old freak. the present "legitimate" blood bath
incarceration of labor, truth and beauty . . . "the dictatorship of money is good. the
   dictatorship
of the bourgeoisie, this is good. the dictatorship of poverty and terror, this is good."
Thats the lies the rulers' mouthpieces spout. The cackle slobber screech of madness
in power. They preach that the absolute control of our lives by the owners of the factories,
the absolute control of our lives by the owners of money, the absolute control over our
   lives
by the owners of the land. that bloody clique of fiends, their parrot mouthpieces claim is
just. But listen, we are the producers of wealth. the factories land and money are created
by the creators, the workers, the laborers in the mills, on the land, it is the people who
must own what shd be owned. What creates food and clothing and shelter for the Great
Majority must be owned by that great majority. The Workers must own what is necessary
for the whole of society to live. There is enough wealth for everybody, the world is
literally unimaginably rich, yet the masses of people are landless paupers with nothing
to sell but the muscle in their arms. We call for the dictatorship of the producers.
The absolute control and ownership by the creators of value itself. The total control
of society by the majority, the multinational working class. The proletariat in modern
dress. Who must lead the masses of us, with a revolutionary vanguard party at the helm
guided by science, guided by the science, the science of marxism-leninism-mao tse-tung
thought. Ask us what the party taught? Marxism-Leninism-Mao tse-tung thought. Speak
   of
the dictatorship, until you understand it. Explain the dictatorship until you're behind it.
Fight for the dictatorship until it is reality. The dictatorship of the proletariat, the
absolute control of the state by the working class, the majority.
\								You need to say that
								You need to hear that
								not be scared of that

           the goal of our revolution is so the people can rule
           the goal of the revolution is so the people can rule
           the ultimate goal of socialist revolution is so the great majority
                    of the people
                    the masses
                    of people
                    can rule

           This is the dictatorship of the proletariat
           the total domination of society by the working class

           you need to hear that
           you need to talk about that
           you gonna have to fight for that

the dictatorship of the proletariat
think about that
the dictatorship of the proletariat

DAS KAPITAL

Strangling women in the suburban bush
they bodies laid around rotting while martinis are drunk
the commuters looking for their new yorkers feel a draft
& can get even drunker watching the teevee later on the Ford
replay. There will be streams of them coming, getting off
near where the girls got killed. Two of them strangled by
the maniac.
There are maniacs hidden everywhere cant you see? By the dozens
and double dozens, maniacs by the carload (tho they *are*
a minority). But they terrorize us uniformly, all over the place
we look at the walls of our houses, the garbage cans parked full
strewn around our defaulting cities, and we cd get scared. A rat
eases past us on his way to a banquet, can you hear the cheers raised
through the walls, full of rat humor. Blasts of fire, some woman's son will stumble
and die with a pool of blood around his head. But it wont be the maniac. These old houses
crumble, the unemployed stumble by us straining, ashy fingered, harassed. The air is cold
winter heaps above us consolidating itself in degrees. We need a aspirin or something, and
pull our jackets close. The baldhead man on the television set goes on in a wooden way
his unappetizing ignorance can not be stood, or understood. The people turn the channel
looking for Good Times and get a negro with a pulldown hat. Flashes of maniac shadows
   before
bed, before you pull down the shade you can see the leaves being blown down the street
too dark now to see the writing on them, the dates, and amounts we owe. The streets too
will soon be empty, after the church goers go on home having been saved again from the
Maniac . . . except a closeup of the chief mystic's face rolling down to his hands will send
shivers through you, looking for traces of the maniacs life. Even there among the
   mythophrenics.

What can you do? It's time finally to go to bed. The shadows close around and the room is
   still
Most of us know there's a maniac loose. Our lives a jumble of frustrations and unfilled
capacities. The dead girls, the rats noise, the flashing somber lights, the dead voice on
television, was that blood and hair beneath the preacher's fingernails? A few other clues

we mull them over as we go to sleep, the skeletons of dollarbills, traces of dead used up
labor, lead away from the death scene until we remember a quiet fit that everywhere
is the death scene. Tomorrow you got to hit it sighs through us like the wind, we got to
hit it, like an old song at radio city, working for the yanqui dollarrrrr, when we were
children, and then we used to think it was not the wind, but the maniac scratching against
our windows. Who is the maniac, and why everywhere at the same time . . .

A POEM FOR DEEP THINKERS

Skymen coming down out the clouds land
and then walking into society try to find out
whats happening—"Whats happening," they be saying
look at it, where they been, dabbling in mist, appearing &
disappearing, now there's a real world breathing—inhaling exhaling
concrete & sand, and they want to know what's happening. What's happening
is life itself "onward & upward," the spirals of fireconflict clash
of opposing forces, the dialogue of yes and no, showed itself in stabbed children
in the hallways of schools, old men strangling bankguards, a hard puertorican inmate's tears
exchanging goodbyes in the prison doorway, armies sweeping wave after wave to contest
the ancient rule of the minority. What draws them down, their blood entangled with humans,
their memories, perhaps, of the earth, and what they thought it could be. But blinded by
sun, and their own images of things, rather than things as they actually are, they wobble,
they stumble, sometimes, and people they be cheering alot, cause they think the skymen
dancing, "Yeh ... Yeh ... get on it. ... ," people grinning and feeling good cause the skymen
dancing, and the skymen stumbling, till they get the sun out they eyes, and integrate the
inhead movie show, with the material reality that exists with and without them. There are
tragedies tho, a buncha skies bought the loopdieloop program from the elegant babble of
the ancient minorities. Which is where they loopdieloop in the sky right on just loopdieloop
in fantastic meaningless curlicues which delight the thin gallery owners who wave at them
on their way to getting stabbed in the front seats of their silver alfa romeos by lumpen
they have gotten passionate with. And the loopdieloopers go on, sometimes spelling out
complex primitive slogans and shooting symbolic smoke out their gills in honor of something
dead. And then they'll make daring dives right down toward the earth and skag cocaine money
whiteout and crunch iced into the statue graveyard where Ralph Ellison sits biting his banjo
strings retightening his instrument for the millionth time before playing the star spangled
banjo. Or else loopdieloop loopdieloop up higher and higher and thinner and thinner and finer
refiner, sugarladdies in the last days of the locust, sucking they greek lolliepops.
Such intellectuals as we is baby, we need to deal in the real world, and be be in the real
world. We need to use, to use, all the all the skills all the spills and thrills that we
conjure, that we construct, that we lay out and put together, to create life as beautiful
as we thought it could be, as we dreamed it could be, as we desired it to be, as we knew it

could be, before we took off, before we split for the sky side, not to settle for endless meaningless circles of celebration of this madness, this madness, not to settle for this madness this madness madness, these yoyos yoyos of the ancient minorities, Its all for real, everythings for real, be for real, song of the skytribe walking the earth, faint smiles to open roars of joy, meet you on the battlefield they say, they be humming, hop, then stride, faint smile to roars of open joy, hey my man, what's happening, meet you on the
   battlefield
they say, meet you on the battlefield they say, what i guess needs to be discussed here
   tonight
is what side yall gon be on

CLASS STRUGGLE

Years ago we both swore oaths, with another,
of revolution. You, malcolm & I, one night
in a room at the waldorf. Where you had come as
ambassador from new afrika, when the fumes
of revolution 1st opened our nose. Youall
had just kicked out the sheik in zanzibar
took over the radio station and broadcast
that his men had surrendered, and blew all them
away that didnt believe it and came stumbling out
of the barracks. It was just a little after cuba
and the fumes of revolution were blasting open
our nose. We had still not made the motion toward
science, had not yet tracked the long distance to
reality. Close then, we had yet to make a march away
from the most liberal wing of the bourgeoisie, that wing
which paints and poets and snorts cocaine and laughs.
We had yet to make the frantic dash toward our black selves
nor opened up wholly into our afrikan selves, to ready that
strong long striding far distanced arrival at our whole
selves. Malcolm was murdered a month after the three of us met.
And for a generation we slept, so many of us, what that really meant.
We disappeared into islam and kawaida, into sections of truth that each
veered away toward fantasy. Not grasping the fundamental political truths
that the rulers had murdered malcolm behind, nor seeing the cold blooded split
between the black bourgeois preachers of religion and crypto culture and the prophet of
    fire.
But you comrade when I came to your house years later a warm open afrikan cottage
directly across from Mwalimu's place, and you fed our whole party your beautiful wife
    did
and you talked to us of many things and talked to me of revolution, i saw red lenin spread
from wall to wall in your study and still did not understand, nor your openness and
    forrealness
and constant reference to the needs the cause the life the requirements of actual
    revolution.
Now, Babu, brother, in a jail in Tanzania, outside Dar es Salaam, Mwalimu is fighting for
    Human
Rights in SouthAfrika, if President Kaunda will let him, yet you have been sitting in the
dry lifeless box of the prison accused of killing a reactionary who you probably did not
    kill

and you were the fire of the tanzanian revolution, the science, the will to real liberation and
socialism. The marxist brother, the hard Red afrikan, the communist in the cabinet that the
cia drew diagrams about and the afrikan petit bourgeois stared at tensely when your back was
turned. And we have failed you brother, Comrade Revolutionary, because all we've done is
raise this question with your president once in person and once through the mail. We have not
cried out from the tops of the buildings that they are trying to kill scientific communism in Tanzania. We have whispered. We have not screamed and banged on doors, and embarrassed
distinguished persons with "WHAT ARE YOU NIGGERS GOING TO DO ABOUT BABU! WHEN ARE YOU
NIGGERS GONNA CUT SHEIK MOHAMED BABU LOOSE? ARE YOU SO FRIGHTENED OF THE DICTATORSHIP
OF THE WORKERS AND PEASANTS THAT YOU HAVE TO KEEP ITS MOUTHPIECE LOCKED UP!" We have not sd
that brother. We have only whispered through our hands to certain high humanitarians. We have
not kept that vow we made at the Waldorf with you and Malcolm, we have let you down brother.
But take this as the first Warcry of the class, to be repeated and repeated until you are returned to the people. FREE BABU FREE BABU FREE BABU FREE BABU FREE BABU

FOR THE REVOLUTIONARY OUTBURST BY BLACK PEOPLE

The next outburst
by the Black Nation
& the oppressed Black faces thrown
every which way
outside the black belt
home land/banjoes
& lynchings
Tarred flesh
burned flesh
blown minds
non-stop tap dance anthems
Hallelujah muthafuckin god if you got us
here so up yr ass
As salaam alaikum allah
you too (Better for youall you admit it's the capitalist!)
the next outburst
all across the field
of vibrating reality
is a revolutionary
outburst
slaveship life
slave life
peasant life
nation life
ashy city life
all over connected by reason
Kidnapped, subjugated, christianized,
commoditified, stereotyped, packaged
(almost), peasantized, proletarianized
our banjo turns to flights of horns
trumpet piercing sax rolling
Blind Louie Trane
Ojay Ra put up our Dukes
Hyper articulate submerged
moans glimmer bluely
in the real destruction & reemergence
of religion beyond grease lies and bankbook tears

When Bebop showed
all Gods ceased to exist

for the Nation lost in its
new identity
The Isley Brothers
guide the Sly & newly
fallen. Nowhere to go
with this load of weeps
This ton a tears, screams,
& hollers
no where to go
but consider what actually
exists.
The next outburst
          (redlight conked hair explosion
          hangs above the Hudson)

The revolutionary outburst
by black people
be for the liberation of the Black Nation
The capes of our national bourgeoisie
beat in the wind as they tilt from side to side
trying to wave us back
But history fills us completely
History stretches us out of old shape
into new shape
to be in the future
with
This ticking is what passes as time in the
sweaty present
They'll try to kill us for communicating clearly
how the rich people control everything and everybody
so they can stay rich. We are fools to work for them
& keep them fat—but what
choice do we have
work for them
starve
or revolt
Make Revolution!
At this moment the forces are building
the sharp heavy hatchet
of the Black Liberation Movement
The gigantic sledge hammer

of The Black Liberation Movement
hoisted and swung in silence
the sun can catch a purple muscle
tensing
Across the field, a living map, other streams
pour toward the exercising bloods
It is a spectrum of motion, a spectrum
of light bent by particular changes
We are for the revolutionary outburst by black people
We are poised in gradual ascendance to that rising
But that next come up we all go down
The whole of humanity focused in America
We all get down
The vibration that predicts the Black Explosion
describes the explosion of all the people
The outburst that creates the new system

We are for the revolutionary outburst by Black People
      The Liberation of the Black Nation
We are for the revolutionary outburst by all the People
      The freeing of America from bourgeois rule
Not just an out burst, but the steel burning fire of
      The Peoples' War
      The violent birth process
         of Socialism!

POETRY FOR THE ADVANCED

INTRODUCTION

The history of the working-class movement in all countries shows that the better-situated strata of the working class respond to the ideas of socialism more rapidly and more easily. From among these come, in the main, the advanced workers that every working-class movement brings to the fore, those who can win the confidence of the laboring masses, who devote themselves entirely to the education and organization of the proletariat, who accept socialism consciously, and who even elaborate independent socialist theories. Every viable working-class movement has brought to the fore such working-class leaders, its own Proudhons, Vaillants, Weitlings, and Bebels. And our Russian working-class movement promises not to lag behind the European movement in this respect. At a time when educated society is losing interest in honest, illegal literature, an impassioned desire for knowledge and for socialism is growing among the workers, real heroes are coming to the fore from amongst the workers, who, despite their wretched living conditions, despite the stultifying penal servitude of factory labor, possess so much character and will-power that they study, study, study, and turn themselves into conscious Social-Democrats—"the working-class intelligentsia."

—"A Retrograde Trend in Russian
Social Democracy,"
Collected Works, Vol. 4, V. I. Lenin
(Progress Publishers, Moscow)

A POEM FOR ANNA RUSS AND FANNY JONES

An old story—the world—old now for us who was once a young stormy buck railing railing
even the tone sounding inside for the change of things that we never knew, was heavy, it
shimmered colors nobody ever seen. Yet it had to be run down finally. it had to control
and discipline itself, it had to make absolute sense, and pt out clearly what it meant.
Who were its enemies, this consciousness is what I mean, this feeling abt life, reality,
is a people's, is a nation's, is a link tho, to a billion people everywhere trying to live
and understand. Your skin scraped off so the moonlight stings, so the swish of bird's wings
brings a message to the brain. Where the perception mashes continuous a message from
 the
world. A link with the billions. This is the world. We are in it. We can live and survive
at a higher level. We can advance all life to higher ground. And the quiet grandmothers
 died
and went to "heaven" could take note of the same feeling cause that's what they had to
 mean
if the metaphysical cloak their times had draped on their world was translated. There is a
better life, but its in the world, in the lives of the people, we just have to struggle, we
just have to care and take care and study, we just have to fight some more people's wars.
That wd be the hymn underneath, we will meet again on higher ground. That all society
 will
be raised to higher ground, a more advanced life. And that feeling has burned in me since
the dawn of my life. That all of us cd meet on higher ground. And now it has to come out
very straight and clear. That this is not possible without violence and revolution, that
there is no higher ground possible without the destruction of real evil which is capitalism
and the rule of the rich. That the rule of the tiny minority must be crushed by the billions
and this is the clear message that has to come out, that cannot be hidden with lyricality
and mysticism or vagueness and romanticism. It has to be said, and having said it, the
 monsters
conspire to kill those who dare make it plain. They huddle and plot our repression and
 pain. But
just like the old stories grandmama, that aint no big thing, we learned how evil wd act in
Sunday School, and how the people, the righteous, wd always win!

SAYONARA, TOKYO

August 1976   *Conference on S. Korea*

Coming in
Coming out
Like everything else
What is coming into
being
what
is going
out.

We had come here to help with the liberation
of South Korea. Another fascist
put up by the USA. Like Nguyen Thieu
Lee Kwan Yew, Lon Nol
& a buncha other savage nuts
held in power by the magnetism of the "greenback"
& the lead spit of the machine gun.
Pak Jung Hee of the ROK pushes
& pushes his people past the brink of necessity
"Korean Democracy" the whole country a dungeon
the whole of the people
in chains. & why? So
a handful of maniacs can make money off
the people's misery

Many people came together here
to commit themselves to help the heroic Korean people
talking democracy, & unity & the overthrow
of the fascist Pak regime. Some stray idealists
tried to turn things around insisting wild beasts
cd be sung to sleep with sweet pleas
or money mad maniacs made to work
for the people & that this cd be done
peacefully
But this mist of fantasy
cannot hold. For the crazy dogs
do not dance because
we think about music
They must be butchered by the people

who turn their misery & anger into
knives & hatchets
& hack off the slobbering hounds'
heads. Tyranny, fascism, capitalism
will not die because they are bad
but because
we kill them

& let no one tell you to feel sorry
you must kill,
comrades, to have something clean
you must eliminate
the dirt.
It is clear
It is necessary
It is scientific. It is
waiting
to be done!

>					August 16, JAL 006
>					Tokyo to New York

REPRISE OF ONE OF A.G.'S BEST POEMS!

America existed in

           its ribboned
           columns
           in its matrix
           of screams
              & pioneers

           (to the end!
           to the max!

      America existed

      in its own memory

      as its own vanity

      a butcher in a cowboy suit

      in its columbus' myths

      told by Flip Wilson

      they sd, "flip
           flip
           flip"

        ac-dc

        in the dark

        teeth glowed green

     America had money belts that

      glowed green in the

        dark like Flip

           Wilson's teeth

   Flip Wilson's teeth were gold

    pharaohs hung around

    Jesse Jackson's neck

 a pioneer of the late 20th century

   inspiring Morgan think tanks to new creativity

   on ways to trick Bloods

  Peanut jesus Jimmy riding niggers like ashy rolls royces

America Warhol

America Starsky

America rhythm hats thrown up

& they bleed from straw murders, stingy murders, homburg murders

 tyrolean, snapbrim

 & cowboy hat murders

America an imperialist bandit bleeding out the bowels

 wipe its ass w/ a dollar bill

 wipe its ass w/ a Latino peasant

 wipe its ass w/ yo' mamma you let it

In its bicentennial jism

In its death penalty enema

America

Allen Ginsberg sd

"Go fuck yrself w/ yr

Atom Bomb"   —and yr doing

                              it!!

He is one of yr prophets

    blind & crazy

    metaphysical

    petty bourgeois

    intellectual

    "strummin & hummin

    all day"

        the image of the

        happy

        slave

We wade in the water

        America

        America

We wade in the bleeding

We wade in the screaming

    in the unemployment

    in the frustrated wives

    & impotent husbands

    of the/ dying middle

    class,

       in the anger of its

       workers

       its niggers

       its wild intelligent

       spics

       its

       brutalized

       chicanos

       its women out of work, again

Hymn poem for the passing into

       for the change into

             the transformation

America

       yr going Communist

       yr bourgeoisie oppose it

       & their sell out lackie

       fools

       but yr going communist

             America

             Maybe you need to be

             investigated

             for yr unamerican

             activities

                    Yr shielding

                    Commies

                    I'm a red pinko Commie

                    A Communist

                    a Marxist-Leninist

                    Whose ideology is

                            Marxism-Leninism-Mao Tse-tung
                    Thought!

America, Communism is the only way

    for you

  the only way

    for the world

Capitalism

    is dying

& its killing, has killed,

    too many

    already.

Private property is a metaphysical concept

the land, the wealth, belongs

to the people

"Better Red, let a small group of others,

 be Dead"

I'm going to stop calling you, "America"

   Yr the United Snakes—alright

              United States

   A.G. thought you was "America"

   because that was yr myth-name

     yr promise

      yr Golden

    name,

      yr name of

       collectivity

         & Communism

But the rest of us know yr the U.S.A.

    the United States

      of America

    The Capitalists' Shangri-La

Explosion is yr middle & "maiden"

name. Violence

yr mid-wife.

      Explosion will birth you into

        Change

           Dont think the Rebellion 60's

        got you over. The poverty pimp

        Frankensteins & Jack-Leg Politicians

        will not stop the flow of "is"!

You got to do it

    & go through

      it

  Yeh—even you, America—got to change

    even you, America—got to change

[America -merica merica

  merica merica merica

  merii -caaaaaaa]

run the word to yr

rich folks

to the swine perverts

who run you

& if they tell you, "Over they dead bodies"

        tell them

        its the only

        way!

MALCOLM REMEMBERED (FEB. '77)

Malcolm
Callin you back thru
years
12 years
Murder
ago
12 years Cia
ago
12 years
Elijah
ago

Malcolm
some of us
turned
Communist
finally
the motion
has deepened
from the unknown
to the known
the perceptual
to the rational

            Malcolm
            yr trip to afrika
            yr sunni turning
            yr chickens home
            to shield themselves
            from fire, real hypocrites
            wheel white schoolmarms into the roxbury mosque
            & name their dying structures after you, dear friend

Malcolm, comrade
many of us have changed
but the masses build their iron strength
despite Roy Innis openly supporting racists
or Floyd McKissick, just plain sick, for short
(very short) caught slowly unzippering Nixon's fly

or Sammy Davis, quickly unzippering it, and plunging in there
all 6 inches of him, grin first

Malcolm, comrade
forgive my pornographic bitter thoughts
but we still live in the pornography center
of the world

& some of us
have changed

Robt Wms is quiet now
& Bobby Seale has disappeared

Huey skipped to Cuba
with a cloud of weird charges (I mean amongst
the people)
over his head

Rap just got out of a behavior modification center
whispering of the sunni. Comrade they killed you before
yr final motion. When you returned
& sd that religion shd be put in the closet
because already
you saw it went further
than God
that God
cd not stop Rockefeller
only the trained trigger fingers
of the millions
guided by revolution

you saw it went beyond black &
white, and exposed the bourgeoisie
even the spooky ones rewriting the bible
with cadillacs and bean pies

In the tempest of fire
the torrents and hurricanes

of fire
we learned
from you. Comrade worker, comrade
Leader. Friend and visionary. Seeing

further ahead
than most of us.
Of vietnam, in the 60's
you sd, just black pajamas
and a bowl of rice
is all they've got,
but they'll drive
Uncle Sam's cold ass
out.

And yes,
And yes,
Ho sd so, the real
dragons flew
out of the prisons
and the revolutionary tumult
goes
on

But some of us
comrade,
have changed.
The negative aspect
dominating, turned us
into our opposites
   Karenga mouthing social democrat cultural opportunism
   in the same slickmohair/buba suits, like a highschool all-
   star suddenly turned middleage, peddling varsity letters
   to workers, telling 11th grade jokes to scientists!

Carmichael, my man, a credit card
panafrikanism, deifying eclecticism
and pettybourgeois subjectivism, raising
Nkrumah, only to tear him down. I'm sorry
brother, America, is my home. And the black
belt, the afro nation. Fire like malcolms
runs thru us, our history and life, run

thru us, but we built this thing from the
ground up, and we'll grab control by and by
But Malcolm, brother, comrade
some of us
turned
communist too
there's yr fire
lighting flashes
out our eyeballs

And we're still
in the street
with you

Yeh, big Red,
some of us, turned
Big Red too

But there's terror
like Eldridge
carrying his bakuninism
to the end

They withheld the dope
of american
applause
and the dirty lumpen
hippy
sold us
out

Young Tony Vargas who played in the toilet years ago
is now huggy bear
on television
now he's in the toilet
for real

the state destroyed the panthers because of their incorrect line
the young lords made it to marxism but destroyed themselves
with dogmatism, left opportunism, urged forward by the same
assassin agents that killed featherstone, and fred hampton,
    & you

the cp-usa talks their same lies, but they got some more black
    folks
fronting it off
movie star angela
the cp's shirley chisholm
shirley nominates rocky
angela nominates gussy
the people build their steel anyway beneath
but we dont have a party
comrade, malcolm
we dont have a marxist-leninist
party
We know how you were moving
We are your students, that's how we got here studying
Marx & Mao and Engels & Lenin, thats what got us to Hoxha
& Stalin, following you comrade, and the fire path you made.
But we dont have a party
comrade,
& when they killed you
it left a double vacuum
No communist party, no national
leadership, and tho the fires reached the base of heaven itself
(which is a subsidiary of General Motors)
our spontaneity cooled it out, the fact that there was no
science
that we
understood
we took it on guts emotion
and love
necessary
but not
sufficient

we needed need
science
we needed need
marx
engels
lenin
stalin
mao tse-tung
to sustain us
& guide us

build tactics
& strategy
principally
a party,
   the party
   of a new
   type,
      this is our central
      task.

           Comrade, I have nothing more
           to ask,
                  you gave
                  everything
                  as must all
                  revolutionaries
                  we still learn from you
                  we are trying to stand
                  on your shoulders
                  black people will
                  be free
                  working people will
                  be free
                  the very sidewalks
                  turn to fire
                            beneath the bourgeois's feet

Summed up, this is what yr whole life meant:
"Fight, Fail, Fight Again, Fail Again, Fight
Again . . . Till their Victory. That is the logic
of the people." Rebellion, betrayal, rebellion
betrayal, and yet again rebellion, till revolution
this is what your life meant, this is yr unfailing teaching
When we say, "Malcolm X," it fills us with this meaning.
Until our victory, Comrade Malcolm, until
our victory!

AN AMERICAN OPPRESS STORY!

Remember Howdy Doody?
Well, he grew up
& became/ Jimmy
    Carter,
    millionaire,
    capitalist,
    peanut pusher—

& he's gonna ask you to settle
for peanuts
(as leading representative
of the extreme left wing
of the SS)

Instead of absolute change
which is revolution
Howdy will beg you to
settle for
peanuts

Nix Him

LIKE, THIS IS WHAT I MEANT!
—for Sparky

Poetry makes a statement
       like everything
       like everything poetry
       makes a statement

Poetry is a being of words
      a being of language flicks
      produced by the life
      of (DAH da da Dah!)
    "ThE pOeT"
But here is where we differ
from Funk & Wagnalls, Empson
     Thaddeus Dustface
     & the rest of assorted bourgeois functionaries
     of the inherited
        decaying
        superstructure

"Take Class Struggle
   as the Key Link", sd Mao, "Act according
              to the past principles"

So that even in our verse
The roar of raging mass
is heard

So that
even in our
  verse
     the struggle
     erupts. the 4 fundamental contradictions
       in the world
       today
       Leap out in
       relief,

         So that even
         in our verse

we move by vibrations with the unstoppable
masses, advancing
the
Chairman sd,
"Wave upon
Wave,"
So that even
in our verse, we are transported
by the billion voiced mass
chanting revolutionary slogans
as they sweep forward to
        crush
        the piss faced
          bourgeoisie

"Countries want Independence
Nations want Liberation
People want Revolution," Chairman Mao
                            has sd
        & we "act
        according
        to the past principles"

Poetry must sing, laugh & fight
Poetry must reveal, probe and light
Poetry must take class struggle
        as the key link
        must remold its world view
        to take up the struggle
        for the mighty
        working
        class

Poetry must see as its central task
        building
          a Marxist-Leninist
            Communist Party
            in the USA

So that even in our verse
we wage ideological struggle over political
line

engage in struggle
guided by M-L-M

to get a program for a party
and a party for our
program
So that
even in
our verse
our song

we are working for
the change
no,
    this aint strange

So that even
even in our verse, our poetry
                  our song

      we are building human
           explosion

    to smash
    capitalism
    to smash
    to smash
    capitalism
    to smash
    to smash
    capitalism

So that even in our verse
the irresistible tide of revolution
is unleashed
yes
unleashed

So that even
  in our verse
this Red Explosion
  is unleashed

Yeh
unleashed

So that even
  in our
  verse
  even in
  our dancing   } (repeat as song)
  even in
  our song
  yeh
  in our pure lover song

REVOLUTION!!!

THE "RACE LINE" IS A PRODUCT OF CAPITALISM
(for my brothers & sisters in the O.P.P. & O.P.R.P.)

Today, there's no need for backwardness
among us,
we all went thru the 60's, I'm talkin to you;
veterans and 40ish swifties, been here for
a while. You mature folks, young in the 50's
when King was doin
his thing, and Trane was just
goin to Miles
& Malcolm was
convincing Elijah
that the Nation needed a
newspaper.
        You know,
    some of the things
        that've gone down. Even the purely perceptual (what
is that?)
the purely
surface, fragmented, splintered
consciousness
know
know
something
went down, 50's to 60's, to now,
in the
70's, know
    know
  something

there's no need
    no need
    for backwardness
    yet there is always
    uneven development
even among the masses, the advanced
        the average
        the backward
            , but so much has gone down.
The advanced
have moved past
the past, the old okeedoke

have climbed on over, put down,
the new
okeedoke

Makin It In America, that got
put down
exposed, by time of korea
the man in the gray flannel
suit, cd do nothing about
the stupidity of straightup
america, cdnt cool out eisenhower
or Eastland, people gettin blown away
with waterhoses or burned in ditches at
midnight, dude went on drinking martinis
talkin gibberish on commuter specials
sniffin the mattress to see who the woman
in the gray flannel suit was sleeping
with.
Bombed out in the suburbs sounding dumb like
John Updike, or one of them other
dikes
    the advanced put that down, squinted
sort of, and kept splittin
kept searchin—
Bohemia Trip, wild and woolly
in america,
the sons and daughters of the slaves and immigrants
hugging and sugging allured wif theysefs
so special
and hip, a purely
hedonistic
trip
aint it about pleasure
was the
line
aint it
aint it
and the me, yeh, me me me
them,
of everything

what they called
Beat,

/ 299

the thump of the heart maybe
loud against the staleness
the
dead
ness
of the beastamerica, dimly perceived
as a corny midwestern middleamerican rich peasant
traumatized by commerce, and a regular paycheck
not to grow
nothin
so prices could stay
high

Howl, then,
was the name of the
claim, to sense, wild out, drop out, high and haid stretched
anything but
silent and stiff we had found out it was not the land of the free
smoked bush, nutmeg, opium, and homeruns
shot scag, cocaine, procaine, took magic mushrooms,
snorted the girl, shoved glass cachets of amyl nitrate
up our nose

& old grand dad, boilermakers, beer & booze,
fight anybody
do anything
sleep with anybody
animal, vegetable or mineral
the roar inside went on,
the roar, the roar, went
on,
and the world, itself, stretched and
changed,
it
changed.

One did split
into two
Malcolm left
Elijah
    Rob Wms
left
Roy Wilkins

The Panthers and Sncc
split
the artists
got thrown out
the black house
which was engineered by the traitor anarchist jesus freak cleaver
one did
split
into two
  and the advanced went away from . . .
  left again
  were not there, you sd what about that book, that dude, what
you told me,
are you . . .
  no,
  I checked it
  no,
  it had some things,
  there is a negative
  and a positive
  I took
  what was there

but then, that didnt, it cdnt, answer
everything. . . .

We went back to afrika. When Malcolm died, and before that
the CPUSA, left a hole in our soul, a gap in our rap, a vacuum
into which flowed the kept out ignorance of antiscience.

We had to go back
the rulers sd we had no human life, no soul, no history, no
culture, and black, we sd black, black, meant, we rejected
the bleached nigger dwarf, reading the newyorker magazine
with his head inserted deep in elizabeth taylor's womb.

we were
we did, we are, we screamed our names, black black black
stretched ourselves, malcolm and trane blowing purple black fire
out our nose and eyes
black, we sd
black black!

And yeh, black did, was, is, but see, look, see, can you
in the swirl, the real world, is burning, its there, all
its crazy motion, and contradiction
we tried to go back in impossible subjective timespace culture warp
and stand the static life of old times up
it can not,
all is, the only constant
is,
yeh yeh yeh, change!

   the afroamerican people move in the west,
part of the menacing fist the people grow
• in their final heads
Our nation in the black belt south
chains draped around us everywhere,
the smoke pours out our nose, our eyes
turn up, roll, when we sense the absolute
reality, of our oppressors neck flying thru
space and time, in perfect trajectory, no
matter the twists and turns, directly into
our stranglers mitts.

Say did you know, brothers, sisters, did you hear
about the parade the long long line, of nigger servants
of evil. Did you know that Belgian Congo had changed to
Zaire, and Mantan Moreland Mobutu starves our people still
Or intellectual Eric Wms, after fighting against the rule
of the white man, the british colon, had took up oppression
on his own, linked his hot thing to the same imperialism
and trinidad moaned under his bullshit
there are fools tell you the bullets black reactionaries
kill with
dont hurt
ha ha ha
(laugh time . . . bitter bloody, heat ready
ha ha ha

But there's no need
for backwardness
look at it, look
the advanced, pick up
their tents
they see the lies, the deathwish

there is my brother coming toward me smiling
smile brother smile, his hand, is held straight
out. He is clean, standing straight, he tells me
this terror life, is good. And yet a line of bodies
swing
in slow distortion
a line of dead workers
sewed to a steel wire strung up from coast to
coast
the bodies rotting
swinging back
and forth
the nigger laughs a screechy clown
pointing as he runs to
the press conference accepts the
reward as the first puerto
negro
chicano asian
woman, trade unionist
to get rolled up
in yet another of
Daddy Overkill's "success" reefers
A pageant of those flashy death scenes
moan by us at supersonic speeds, blood
come down
like rain
how your stomach feel
you dig its
your blood
the bloated vampire
spit it up

A pageant of our flashy
deaths,
in places all over
the world.
Took off, shot down,
locked up, sent out
or bought and sold in quiet little rooms
where the tea's very good.

We learned, the advanced
in the dim swim of speed hits

   rapes, assassinations
   muggings, all, pax vobiscum, in the name
   of the father the son and the holy
   ghost
   (Bullshit piled up into the WayGonesphere)

They people pray to Jesus, Allah, Buddha, Jehovah, Ra, Haile
Selassie, and even Rev. Ike and other poverty pimps, and still
they poor,
   The Advanced were never there, and if they were,
   the wind of their motion, shredded the "believers" eyes
   they moved so fast
      Think of Malcolm!

We saw a line of niggers,
of any bodies, long as the whole shit was stacked wrong,
as long as the big paw of capitalism leaned on it
on them
on us
on all of what there was, it soured, tilted, wrecked,
and so distorted
black hands killed Malcolm and Amilcar
Cabral/ Nat Turner, Vesey, Prosser
turned in by niggers
like Andrew Young
& Kenneth Gibson

We saw, we moved, we learned, sometimes
our heads
covered with blood
we learned
we saw the revolutionaries
charging, fighting, struggling
and winning
around the world. We Saw
While we talked of partial truths, and mistakes
While we memorized The Seven Principles, and lit candles
for Kwanza
while we posed as reality innocent tapes
quoting social democrat negro buddhists
posing as, pontificating as, strutting and
wenching, as, black

The race line held by the suffering middle class
and the ruling class
as well. Put them together
and shake em up good
you know what you get
America.
Hitlers strutters were pettybourgeois race freaks
shopkeepers martyred by Imperialism, Robber-Boxing.

Can you envisage the fat professors grown to Blk Studies Profoundity
Who will stand you down, even on the ramparts with Dupont no longer
able to live better through capitalism's chemistry, shouting Afrikans
created Christianity, Beethoven was Black, White boys cant swing, trying
even then to finish out their last incredible essay on Ghetto
Polysyllabic Symbolism & Reference To Ritual, In The Phrase Suck Out
My Ass Till You Get Shitty Drunk, And Stagger Back For More, As Heard
Passing The Alleys of Philadelphia In a Late Model Mercedes Benz!

No, not with them,
they go down, as all the ugly shit
will go,
strapped, right dead,
with the rulers
Let them be sididdy, hincty, 400, girl friends, turtles, Alpha
Kappa, Q, Delta, AKA,
in the flame of the bourgeois's slaughter
the destruction of their world
let all that shit, let them be screaming
Ebony, AfroSheen, "more Parks Pork Sausages Mom!,"
North Carolina Mutual, Supreme Life, Even
as they fry with the biggies, their true Gods,
I M P E R I A L I S M !!!

There's no need for backwardness
let it go, let the race line go,
our resistance to terror is Revolution
It will sweep the whole slate clean
it will right these centuries of wrongs
It will set the conditions for the destruction
of racism, and women's oppression, end forever
the ancient rule of the minority, and *every* form
of slavery
Come from the 30's, grew in the 40's, shaped in the

50's, fought in the 60's, its time now to reap the harvest
of consciousness, of raised
understanding. There's no need
for backwardness, if you claim to be
the advanced. Uneven development, yet
there are the advanced, whose grasp
of the science will create the instrument
of all our liberation. The people
have no weapon, but organization.
It is class struggle that is the key link
the people grasp as the makers
of history. It is class struggle,
and revolution, that raise the whole world up!
Spit out the rulers' narcotic teaching
then spit out the rulers
themselves.
Humanity is divided, only by
oppression.

ALL REACTION IS DOOMED!!!

Why is it they want revolution
to take a back
seat
revolution wont
take no back
seat

Back seats wont be around long anyway
just collective
seats
& why they want revolution
to come in sideways
because they holding
bullshit up
with they words
or lives

Because they holding bullshit up
w/ they words and they
lives
w/ they words
or they
lives

& words unconnected
w/ reality
is a hurricane
of bullshit
they want revolution
to take a back seat
& revolution wont

It'll run over
them
They crying lie time
     funny time
       eruption tears they
       new shoes off plants
       them in their mouth
       ass first.

    Ripped, by

        Ripped, by Revolution

& they want revolution
to take a back seat
to not be said
or only indirectly mumbled

amidst the bloody graverobbed
frustration
amidst the jagged dead people skies
       teeth tear throats
       drown lie words
                in blood

They want revolution to take
    a back seat
But revolution will
    not
Independent of anyone's
    will
    revolution
    continues

    They want
    to stop
    what they cant   (They They)
                                  They

    to back up
    what cannot
    be backed
    up   (They They)
                                They

    to
    silence
    what roars holes
    in the old
    world
They want revolution

to take a back
seat They They They—They
Who? They—the ignorant They
the cowardly, but mainly They
the bourgeoisie & their criminal lackies
in all colors, shapes
sizes & sexes
bureaucrats, aristocrats
renegades of various stripes
sellouts, traitors, weaklings of
diverse types
opportunist dung
maggot spies against
the people
selling sheep
tickets
babbling about peace,
when we need class war
trying to make collaboration
sound profound
or funny or hip or smart
They try to make revolution
take a back seat, no seat
because they're upholding
This! They're upholding This!
Try to eliminate
revolution
or they're hip
& say, "just so
the bourgeoisie
can dig
it
it's OK
We dig it
but so many
ain't ready for
it," but ready
  or not, independent
  of anyone's
  will—

  You might not dig it
  but you cant

stop
it!
They want revolution to
   take a back seat
   to get under the covers
   & be quiet
   to sit by the window & wait
   till syphilis rots
   Rocky's brain
   & the bourgeoisie collectively die
   from the weight of their
   enormous filth. Meanwhile
   they grinnin skinnin finding
   new spectacular ways to Tom,
   Jeff & bullshit
   the people
   But there is no quiet wait
   at a rainy doorway
   for the universal metaphysical heart attack—

Independent of anyone's will
Revolution pushes the world
forward! It will not take a
back seat. It will not allow
itself to be hid, mumbled, disguised
it lashes
out
    it raises
up
      it transforms
      millions!
            It will not
              take a back seat
            It cannot be
              silenced
            It cannot be dodged
              or
              sidestepped
"The world's in great disorder
A good thing for
the people"

Socialdemocrat formal nervous laughter
cant stop it

The super powers
cant stop it
Nixon's xmas dracula bombings
didn't
Watergate
didn't
Kennedy's carrot
Mitchell's stick
   all the ex sncc niggers
   working for foundations
   being councilmen or
   high line political hustlers
   cant stop it

   Floyd McKissick @ Soul City
   cant stop it

   Sammy Davis swapping spit w/
   "Tricky Dick"
   cdn't stop it

Revolution wont take no
   back
   seat
   It's
   an
   irresistible
   tide
   irresistible
   tide
   sweeping the world

   wont take no
   back seat
   wont
   be
   put down
   people ready for it now
      ready for it
      ready for it
      now
      Struggling

      for it Strugglin
      for it
      now
      Can't be
      put down
      cant be
      put in no
      back seat
Yr lies aint gon stop it
Yr jive traitor copouts
      aint gon stop it

Bullshit Jackson w/ his suede coat
    attache case & new hat
    tryin to get over in hollywood
    new york
    or rome
    cant stop it

Bullshit Romano w/ his sweater leather jacket
    contract w/ Universal
    Magazine Swagger
    his new flick opening soon
    aint gon do it

J. Bullshit Seidel, pheenom on the
    silver gridiron, stuffs
    slap dunks, flyin
    toward the
    hoop
    caint

All lineups of toms, in step sly anglos on
wall street. Greenwhich connecticut
cocktail crossbleats
cant

Wm Buckley's viper forked tongue
    sliding &
    darting
    with his cunning
        lingo

Let's nickname him
Cunning Lingo
But that wont stop nothin'

I in my weakness, slowness, right opportunist
   error is my name,
   cant stop it
   cant put it in no
   back seat

Nor Flash "Lefty" who purgest everyone
   even throws people
   out they house
   opposing empiricism
   but not dogmatism

No "Gang of Four," nor any other vicious minorities
can stop it
nor derail it shooting past
reality

Capitalist Roaders
   cdnt stop it w/ their
   pragmatic clap trap
Liu Shiao Chi
Lin Piao & Confucius
Wang Ming
Li Li-san
Chen Tu-hsiu
nor Chiang Kai-shek
cd make it take no
back seat

Fat bald head traitor Khrushchev
led a new bourgeoisie
to restore capitalism
in the land of
Lenin
Destroy him in effigy daily
& destroy that system wherever it is
   But he cant stop it
   Cant make revolution
   take a back seat

nor his replica partner
Brezhnev
him neither
People making revolution
against their Social Imperialist ass now

Trotsky cdn't & Trotskyites
those bedbugs made of vomit
    they cant neither
    a petty bourgeois trend
    in the western industrial
    countries
        Fool Trotsky
        Fool Bukharin
        Fool Martov
        Fool Kautsky
        Include Fool Hall & Fool Angela
        They cdnt stop it
        Second International
        cdnt stop it
Hitler, Franco, Hoover
  nor Pak Jung Hee
    nor you
    nor me
cant make revolution
take a back
  seat

Nothing
  can
It's why things are born
why the new replaces
the old
why there is no oppression
w/o resistance
no down
w/o up
People of the 3rd world
leading the attack
against the Carter-Brezhnev Imperialist
Clique
& working people all over
working people

everywhere
jaws tightening
see the truth
of what
Chairman
Mao sd.
"Cast aside illusion
Prepare
to
Struggle"
Know nothing comes
in soft puffs
of fantasy
food
from the
earth
coal from the
mountains
fish from the
sea
s'work
& struggle
study & consistency
You afraid of work
sd Lenin
you'll never
reach the
truth
The energy
is the commitment
the "Spirit Reach"—
but be in
Shape!
The energy
is the
commitment
The motion of "will be" to
"is."

Revolution
    wont take
        no back
            seat

Revolution
   wont be
      put down
Nor mumbled, dodged, dished, tricked
outlasted, defeated, filed, bought off,
shot, exiled, returned in a cheap suit,
courtesy of the FBI, screaming abt it
found Jesus (like J. Edgar Cleaver)
Revolution
will not be
denied
It will not die or
   go away
It will not
   take a back
      seat
No one can escape it
Revolution is the burst of Life
into
Life
& while there *is* Life
There is
Revolution
Commit yrself to it
Commit yrself to it
Remold yr world view
Take up the struggle of Humanity
to perfect
itself

CHINATOWN

Chiang Kai-shek
  ends up
  in China Town
  among the Ghost
      Shadows   (U.S.A.)
He says   Taiwan Falls!
      Somewhere (thissa his son—he col' daid years ago)
      he say
           Somewhere (like the Lie-Opera)
                  You know, "SuuuuuuuuummmmmmWhayyyyyyy
                        rrrr. . . ."
                            Dig?

His son Chiang Ching-kuo
carryin' on, in any kind of weather
Somewhere
he say
There must be some
            where
                  to go   (British lease on Hong Kong
                          expires, 1998)

GO TO HELL MOTHAFUCKA!!! (a chorus
                    of farmers
                    leanin on they hoes
                    outside Taipei
                    give him the nasty finger
                    as the Yanks ease their gunboats
                    on out toward the Pacific, John Wayne
                    having changed into Jimmy Carter who is
                    really Howdy Doody who is really John
                    Dillinger dressed up as Jesus who is
                    mythical but is really Leonid Brezhnev
                    who is really Lucky Luciano, The Son of
                    Sam! Uncle Pervert the Superpower, stirring
                    up   the   hideous   Russian-American   Gangfuck
                      known
                    as World War Three!)
                              That was an aside
                              But right on the money!

Some-where Chiang's son say
The state department brochure
says
Come To The USA
No Commies Over Here Worth Shit!
Set up shop on Canal St.!!
So these dimwits, the big foot of the Chinese people
driven nonstop & deep deep, way up in their ass
cut a tragic swagger (get to that!)
on out and across the sea
invest in scag, hotels, restaurants, some three story
gambling
dens—
    Read the brochure, as they sail
    Read the brochure, comforts them as they "book"
    Read the brochure, heading for the USA

    But it neglects to point out,
    that even in this fortress of imperialism
    capitalism is not here
    to stay!

ON THE MONEY

Ugly Ugly Ugly Ugly Ugly Ugly Ugly Ugly
Ugly Ugly Ugly Ugly Ugly
Ugly Shit
Ugly Shit
Ugly Shit
U.S.
U.S.
U.S.
U.S.

PRES SPOKE IN A LANGUAGE

Pres
    spoke in a language
"of his own." What did he say, between the
horn line
s, pork pie hat
tenor tilted
pres once was a drummer but gave it up cause other dudes was getting
the foxes
while he packed his tomtoms
"Ding Dong," pres sd, meaning
like a typewriter, its the end
of this
line. "No Eyes," pres wd say, meaning
I didn't cdn't dig it, and what it was was
lame, Pres
had a language
and a life, like,
all his own,
but in the teeming whole of us he lived
toooting on his sideways horn
translating frankie trumbauer into
Bird's feathers
Tranes sinewy tracks
the slickster walking through the crowd
surviving on a terrifying wit
its the jungle the jungle the jungle
we living in
and cats like pres cd make it because they were clear they, at least,
had to,
to do anything else.
Save all that comrades, we need it.

INSIDE OUT

Presences, all voices lights touches ideas came in here
We look up
name it, shape it. I have a painting here, it is thousands of
red blotches singing
ducks take off amidst bullet showers
The old woman turns; her eyes out the window silent with the cars
alabama marauding in her head again
a lover's look is all that's left, a word draped
between street signs and the smell of dog
history and the present intertwine like broadway
pornography
a hand is raised, what does it mean, hello, hi?, stop, come back,
I meant to tell you the money came yesterday
whew, yo breath is heav—vie . . .
meanings, picture life, lives, dynamic blood carrying seeing and humming
in the air as I turned I cd see the ball spiroid zooming
what can I tell you, blue pants leather jacket, hat pulled down,
beneath it all a form of order, a base, a life together producing
life. We hold hands in the semidark, so long together, thoughts needed
to be talked and not. We cannot speak and the wind does it for us
bounding past us with its hours.
Zigzag hearts, crisscrossed meaning, souls hooked up and struggle itself.
I've grown old loving a woman and these children. Changing my mind.
Shadows are crossing the street with their people and they have histories
too. Who will be the last person to hear Earth Wind & Fire
the announcer doesnt know. War on the horizon, Storm winter purging.
Beneath it all, the pictures and presences, the constant stops of change,
and life, is life, the doing and being, the materiality of everything
together. (Ha' Mercy!) Scarecrows blown skyhigh in the raging
night. Little babies coming from work just before their funerals. Zoom,
I tell you, Zoom, its fast yeh, Al Green, Louie Armstrong, Pygmies, Nilotic
Negroes just south of Heidelberg, Marx and Coltrane's ancestors, Zoom,
there is just this screaming, this feeling, these presences as pictures of
everything blowing past, whole lives and histories epochs galaxies balloons
trees, you were saying . . . zoom . . . zooom . . . zoomzoomzoom. . . .

AFRO-AMERICAN LYRIC

Star-ar-t wi-ith
they ra-ay-n, yes, star-ar-t wi-ith the ray
ay
nnnn, it can drive you
say
ay
nn, make you think, of all thats been
all thats passed
all that
flows
wont come back
again
Think about what needs to be
needs to be, think about
what needs
needs
to be,
    think about abou-out
    wha- aat nee eee eee ds
    to be. Uhh
    You see that we're not freeeee
    eee
    the nigger in the city hall
    the colored prime minister opens his colored parliament
    place so hip even the rats doin the hustle

Yeh-et
    all of whats needed is grown around us
    all of whats needed is grown within us
    all of whats needed is all of us needing it
all of what's needed
is all of us
all
of
us
    place so hip
    even the rats do'n
    the hustle

Despite its beauty this world is ugly

The ugliest ugly is the social ugly
the horriblest horrible terriblest terrible
Simple shit uh simple shit
uh simple
shit uh
simple
simple
simple
simple
shit
    society's ugly is the graspingclass
    its simple
    shit uh
    see-imm-pull
    see-im-pull
    Seeeeeeeeeee-immmmmmmmmm
       pull
  Some See - im - pull
    shit
Society's ugly, the ugliest ugly
caused by the grasping
class, exploiting
class

There is no super nothing which entitles nobody
to oppress nobody
See-im
pull
Ugly class
exploiting class
owning class
capitalist class
bourgeois class
reactionary class
no super nothing
no mystical nobody
nothing so slick, proper,
out, xtianish or muslimish
it upholds or justifies poverty
aint nothin legitimatizes
this motherfuckin upside down bullshit system
see-empull, uh
uh

nuthin
uh
nuthin
aint nuthin
    see eem pull
    place so hip the rats
    doin the
    hustle
     Aint nuthin
    "How you doin?"
     "Aint nuthin."
    Nobody, no thing eeeeee

     Think about
     what needs
      to beee

what-ut
neeeds
needs
to be
   Despite its beauty, the world is ugly
   The ugliest ugly
   The owning class

   See em- pull

<u>This Is A Communist Poem!</u>

   Think
   Thin nnn kuh
   ooo Think
   bout
     what
   needs
   to bee
All of us everywhere in control
  of what
  we see
   Think
  Study it Study it Study it
   All of us

　　　　Study it
　　　　Think abt
　　what nee eee eed
　　　　to be
　　without struggle
There is no way
　　to be free
Start w/ this dri ii ving
　　rain
Let it drive　　　drive
　　drive
　　you
　　　　say-
　　　　　　ne

| This Is A Communist Poem! |

　　　　An Afro-American
　　　　　　　Lyric
　　　　Despite its beauty beauty
　　　　　　baby
　　　　　　　despite its beauty
　　　　the world society
is very
ugly

There is no super nothin
　　no mystical nobody
　　　　which makes this bullshit
　　　　　　　　　　right

The ugliest
　　ugly
　is the owners
　　　the high class
　　　　　　Like a roach sittin on top a yr muffins
　　　　　　A blood-fat mosquito
　　　　　　whinin and bitin you
　　　　　　summer nights

　　　Like a blue fly buzzing
　　　　　yr sammich

See-   eemple

    A rattlesnake
    lookin at
    yr baby

    a slobberin dog
    standing on yr
    chest
See-immmmmmmm mem mem mem mem
    pull
Start w/
    the ray   ay
        ayn
        yes.
        start with
        this
        ray   ay ay ain
        it can drive you
        sane
    make you think
    of all thats been
    make you think
    of all thats
    passed
    all that flows
    that wont
    come back
    again
Think about
        study study
            do it
            do it
        Be about what needs
            to
            be
            be about
                what
                    needs
                    nee
                    eee
                eee
                eeeeds

yeh, please, right now
> be
> about
> what
> > needs
> to be.

Only revolution
will set us free!

SPRING SONG

      The juice of life, in human terms,
is human, the oak fastens to rising sun, rain beats it healthy
the blows of all shit fiends raging towards us, humans, towards
the past they empty into, as we fight to find a future. We change
before our own eyes, before our very eyes, slow houdinis, venerable
and weathered. This one got a beer belly, where before he war a slick
read sleek young kid. Now sons, suns, all spat from him, left a mark
like Ahab, a streak of Moby-checking on the beardfront. Notches on the
brain for every daring pettybourgeois intellectual he'd gunned down
in a whole country known as OK Corral. Here, the bad guys are no actors
but actual bad b.o. nixon type motherfuckers who must be scatter blasted flat.
There is a swinish really smiling james cagney as rex reed dude who will
tell you even engels is a revisionist, and so that allows him to go on
with his bullshit. And looking into his icebox, strewn with year old butter
and saggy ritz, you dig his line that work is the enemy. Is it your brain
thats sagging beneath yr hips jasper. You is not a german philosopher, long
dead, but a living black comrade counted on by many folks to keep on steppin.
And not just step step half steppin but stridin, like striding, long ground-
hungry, distance-raising strides. The sun behind us, the day turned red. He
lifts his head, off his chest, the wind wakes him cold, the next hurdle
looms, on five, his leg shoots up automatically, and the wind, sun, ground,
sky, shouts of other comrades, the mass of people surging forward too, remind
him of Trane—yeh Trane—you know that solo—Bee Dooo Bee Dooo Dooooo
   Dooo dooo   (Giant Steps)

DOPE

uuuuuuuuu
uuuuuuuuu
uuuuuuuuu   uuu   ray light morning fire lynch yet
uuuuuuu, yester-pain in dreams
comes again. race-pain, people our people our people
everywhere ... yeh ... uuuuu. yeh uuuuu. yeh
our people
yes people
every people
most people
uuuuuu, yeh uuuuu, most people
in pain
yester-pain, and pain today
(Screams) ooowow!   ooowow! It must be the devil
(jumps up like a claw stuck him) oooo wow! oooowow! (screams)

It must be the devil
It must be the devil
it must be the devil
(shakes like evangelical sanctify
shakes tambourine like evangelical sanctify in heat)

ooowow! ooowow! yeh, devil, yeh, devil ooowow!

Must be the devil must be the devil
(waves plate like collection) mus is mus is mus is
mus is be the devil, cain be rockefeller (eyes roll
up batting, and jumping all the way around to face the
other direction) caint be him, no lawd
caint be dupont, no lawd, cain be, no lawd, no way
noway, naw saw, no way jose—cain be them rich folks
theys good to us theys good to us theys good to us theys
good to us theys good to us, i know, the massa tolt me
so, i seed it on channel 7, i seed it on channel 9 i seed
it on channel 4 and 2 and 5. Rich folks good to us
poor folks aint shit, hallelujah, hallelujah, ooowow! oowow!
must be the devil, going to heaven after i die, after we die
everything gonna be different, after we die we aint gon be
hungry, ain gon be pain, ain gon be sufferin wont go thru this
again, after we die, after we die owooo! owowoooo!

after we die, its all gonna be good, have all the money we
need after we die, have all the food we need after we die
have a nice house like the rich folks, after we die, after we die, after we
die, we can live like rev ike, after we die, hallelujah, hallelujah, must be
the devil, it ain capitalism, it aint capitalism, it aint capitalism,
naw it ain that, jimmy carter wdnt lie, "lifes unfair" but it aint capitalism
must be the devil, owow! it ain the police, jimmy carter wdnt lie, you
know rosalynn wdnt not lillian, his drunken racist brother aint no reflection
on jimmy, must be the devil got in im, i tell you, the devil killed malcolm
and dr king too, even killed both kennedies, and pablo neruda and overthrew
allende's govt. killed lumumba, and is negotiating with step and fetchit,
sleep n eat and birmingham, over there in "Rhodesia", goin' under the name
ian smith, must be the devil, caint be vorster, caint be apartheid, caint
be imperialism, jimmy carter wdnt lie, didnt you hear him say in his state
of the union message, i swear on rosalynn's face-lifted catatonia, i wdnt lie
nixon lied, haldeman lied, dean lied, hoover lied hoover sucked (dicks) too
but jimmy dont, jimmy wdnt jimmy aint lying, must be the devil, put yr
money on the plate, must be the devil, in heaven we'all all be straight.
cain be rockfeller, he gave amos pootbootie a scholarship to Behavior
Modification Univ, and Genevieve Almoswhite works for his foundation
Must be niggers! Cain be Mellon, he gave Winky Suckass, a fellowship in
his bank put him in charge of closing out mortgages in the lowlife
Pittsburgh Hill nigger section, caint be him.
    (Goes on babbling, and wailing, jerking in pathocrazy grin stupor)
Yessuh, yessuh, yessuh, yessuh, yessuh, yessuh, yessuh, yessuh, yessuh, yessuh
put yr money in the plate, dont be late, dont have to wait, you gonna be in
heaven after you die, you gon get all you need once you gone, yessuh, i heard
it on *the jeffersons,* i heard it on *the rookies,* i swallowed it
whole on *roots*: wasn't it nice slavery was so cool and
all you had to do was wear derbies and vests and train chickens and buy your
way free if you had a mind to, must be the devil, wasnt no *white* folks,
lazy niggers chained theyselves and threw they own black asses in the bottom
of the boats, [(well now that you mention it King Assblackuwasi helped throw yr ass in
the bottom of the boat, yo mamma, wife, and you never seed em no more)] must
a been the devil, gimme your money put your money in this plate, heaven be
here soon, just got to die, just got to stop living, close yr eyes stop
breathin and bammm-O heaven be here, you have all a what you need, Bam-O
all a sudden, heaven be here, you have all you need, that assembly line
you work on will dissolve in thin air owowoo! owowoo! Just gotta die
just gotta die, this ol world aint nuthin, must be the devil got you
thinkin so, it cain be rockefeller, it cain be morgan, it caint be capitalism
it caint be national oppression owow! No Way! Now go back to work and cool
it, go back to work and lay back, just a little while longer till you pass

its all gonna be alright once you gone. gimme that last bitta silver you got stashed there sister, gimme that dust now brother man, itll be ok on the other side, yo soul be clean be washed pure white. yes. yes. yes. owow. now go back to work, go to sleep, yes, go to sleep, go back to work, yes owow. owow. uuuuuuuuuu. uuuuuuuuuu. uuuuuuuu. yes, uuuuuuu. yes. uuuuuuuuuu. a men

AM/TRAK

1
Trane,
Trane,
History Love Scream Oh
Trane, Oh
Trane, Oh
Scream History Love
Trane

2
Begin on by a Philly night club
or the basement of a cullut chuhch
walk the bars my man for pay
honk the night lust of money
oh
blow-
scream history love

Rabbit, Cleanhead, Diz
Big Maybelle, Trees in the shining night forest

Oh
blow
love, history

Alcohol we submit to thee
3x's consume our lives
our livers quiver under yr poison hits
eyes roll back in stupidness
The navy, the lord, niggers,
the streets
all converge a shitty symphony
of screams
 to come
 dazzled invective
Honk Honk Honk, "I am here
to love
it." Let me be fire-mystery
air feeder beauty."

Honk
Oh
scream—Miles
comes.

3
Hip band alright
sum up life in the slick
street part of the
world, oh,
blow,
if you cd
nigger
man

Miles wd stand back and negative check
oh, he dug him—Trane
But Trane clawed at the limits of cool
slandered sanity
with his tryin to be born
raging
shit
    Oh
    blow,
        yeh go do it
        honk, scream
        uhuh yeh—history
            love
            blue clipped moments
            of intense feeling.
"Trane you blows too long."
Screaming niggers drop out yr solos
Bohemian nights, the "heavyweight champ"
smacked him
in the face
his eyes sagged like a spent
dick, hot vowels escaped the metal clone of his soul
fucking saxophone
tell us shit tell us tell us!

4
There was nothing left to do but
be where monk cd find him
that crazy
mother fucker
    duh duh-duh duh-duh duh
    duh duh
    duh duh-duh duh- duh duh
    duh duh
    duh duh-duh duh-duh duh
    duh duh
    duh Duuuuuuuuuhhhhhh
Can you play this shit? (Life asks
Come by and listen

& at the 5 Spot Bach, Mulatto ass Beethoven
& even Duke, who has given America its hip tongue
checked
checked
Trane stood and dug
Crazy monk's shit
Street gospel intellectual mystical survival codes
Intellectual street gospel funk modes
Tink a ling put downs of dumb shit
pink pink a cool bam groove note air breath
a why I'm here
a why I aint
& who is you-ha-you-ha-you-ha

Monk's shit
Blue Cooper 5 Spot
was the world busting
on piano bass drums & tenor

This was Coltrane's College. A Ph motherfuckin d
sitting at the feet, elbows
& funny grin
Of Master T Sphere
too cool to be a genius
he was instead
Thelonius
with Comrades Shadow

334 /

on tubs, lyric Wilbur
who hipped us to electric futures
& the monster with the horn.

5
From the endless sessions
money lord hovers oer us
capitalism beats our ass
dope & juice wont change it
Trane, blow, oh scream
yeh, anyway.

There then came down in the ugly streets of us
inside the head & tongue
of us
a man
black blower of the now
The vectors from all sources—slavery, renaissance
bop charlie parker,
nigger absolute super-sane screams against reality
course through him
AS SOUND!
"Yes, it says
this is now in you screaming
recognize the truth
recognize reality
& even check me (Trane)
who blows it
Yes it says
Yes &
Yes again   Convulsive multi orgasmic
              Art
              Protest

& finally, brother, you took you were
(are we gathered to dig this?
electric wind find us finally
on red records of the history of ourselves)

The cadre came together
the inimitable 4 who blew the pulse of then, exact
The flame the confusion the love of

whatever the fuck there was
   to love
Yes it says
blow, oh honk-scream (bahhhhhhh - wheeeeeee)

(If Don Lee thinks I am imitating him in this poem,
this is only payback for his imitating me—we
are brothers, even if he is a backward cultural nationalist
motherfucker—Hey man only socialism brought by revolution
can win)
        Trane was the spirit of the 60's
        He was Malcolm X in New Super Bop Fire
        Baaahhhhh
        Wheeeeeee ... Black Art!!!
Love
History
  On The Bar Tops of Philly
in the Monkish College of *Express*
in the cool Grottoes of Miles Davis Funnytimery
Be
Be
Be reality
Be reality alive in motion in flame to change (You Knew It!)
                to change!!
     (All you reactionaries listening
     Fuck you, Kill you
     get outta here!!!)

Jimmy Garrison, bass, McCoy Tyner, piano, Captain Marvel Elvin
on drums, the number itself—the precise saying
all of it in it afire aflame talking saying being doing meaning

Meditations
Expressions
A Love Supreme
(I lay in solitary confinement, July 67
 Tanks rolling thru Newark
 & whistled all I knew of Trane
 my knowledge heartbeat
 & he was *dead*
 they
 said.

And yet last night I played *Meditations*
& it told me what to do
Live, you crazy mother
fucker!
Live!
  & organize
  yr shit
  as rightly
  burning!

CHILD OF THE THIRTIES

Red Rover
Red Rover
I dare you—darkness
I dare, the quest eludes, a halo shineth
it is an advertisement for chastisement
it is a shibboleth of sternness, driven off
He comes down the road from his childhood
He maniacs the world with his eyes
He drives to the center of craziness with his laughter
He vaults the mediocrity of Frazier-fools with his poetic ironies
But there is a world any-way, yes, any any way how. Lord Moves
in Mysterious Ways, back and forth
to the bank. Greasy (From the song "Take It Easy, Greasy, You Got a Long Way to
 Slide"!) emerges as the first Mayor of a major
northeastern city
sliding toward a kind of in
fame
Remember those blue and white cheerleaders and the 1st colored
to leap 2 of them
a yellow boy and girl
like astronauts in a plastic tube
waiting for the ship to land
the flight goes on
monsters be freaking
roy wilkinses be squeaking
fbi be peeking
the people be seeking
he floateth above himself in himself and his feets tap on the pavement
like bill robinson hoofing
with the statue of liberty (our dog)
notice the stirring endings, the ings of things that identifies
all the john wayne propaganda and greek shit fumbling in my gourd
and yet, there is
a witness, a center of knowing
a recognition, eye to eye, off the boat cool
of the new land looked, of the strange and the cold blue of it
of the love there was, and the indians that died, there, and
all
of us
all of the survivors, till today

our red feet chiming as we wobble and stand straight
as we try to be among the strength of this place
despite a worm big as lothar tries to chew our brain up
to turn us into mantan in a unclesam suit
if you knows the place
if you digs the space
you tryin to make this about race
across the world
whipped and whopped
whammed and bammed
the comintern summed it up
nation in the black belt
afroblue fire the sung flag of memories' future victory
democracy and socialism
joe louis turns on roosevelt
Kid Gavilan boloes Brezhnev to his knees
There is a great peace, after the war
great love, after the hatred
Red Rover, Red Rover, can you understand
class struggle
in the night in front of 19 Dey street,
running back and forth
with the game, the summer wind in your face
like the way your hand would reach your toe
with the wood hurdle
passing an 8th of an inch
under your outstretched leg
pass swift comrade, pass swift
the way the everything do
the way the all the things do
the way the world is blew
blue
bluessssss
the space ship passes
earth
planets
among them struggling
perfect this
perfect this
science not dream

/ 339

Long Live Marx, Engels, Lenin, Stalin, Mao Tse-tung
Red Rover
Red Rover
You're over